Victoria

A Love Story

Victoria

A Love Story

WILLIAM C. HAMMOND

Tasora
Minneapolis

Tasora Books
5120 Cedar Lake Road S
Minneapolis, MN 55416
(952) 345-4488
Distributed by Itasca Books

ISBN: 978-1-934690-74-1

This book is dedicated to establishing a scholarship in Victoria's name at the Kansas City Art Institute.

If you find this book meaningful to you, and if you are moved to do so, please make a donation directly to the Kansas City Art Institute, from which Victoria graduated in 1973. All donations are tax deductible and will be used to establish the Victoria K. Hammond Scholarship. Victoria and I are grateful to you for your kind consideration of this request.

Please send your donation to:

Advancement Office
Kansas City Art Institute
4415 Warwick Boulevard
Kansas City, MO 64111

Be sure to specify
"The Victoria K. Hammond Scholarship"
on your check.

Thank you.

When everything is dark, when we are surrounded by despairing voices, when we do not see any exits, then we can find salvation in a remembered love, a love which is not simply a recollection of a bygone past but a living force that sustains us in the present. Through memory, love transcends the limits of time and offers hope at any moment of our lives.

—Henri Nouwen

"The House"

Sometimes on waking, she would close her eyes
For a last look at that white house she knew
In sleep alone, and held no title to.
And had not entered yet, for all her sighs.

What did she tell me of that house of hers?
White gatepost; terrace; fanlight of the door;
A widow's walk above the bouldered shore;
Salt winds that ruffle the surrounding firs.

Is she there now, wherever "there" may be?
Only a foolish man would seek to find
That haven fashioned by her dreaming mind.
Night after night, my love, I put to sea.

—— Richard Wilbur

Acknowledgments

Midway through writing this book a friend commented to me, "This must be such a labor of love, Bill." She was right, of course. Writing this book has indeed been a labor of love. But not just my labor and not just my love. Throughout this process I have been encouraged by more people than I can give proper credit to here. Nonetheless, the individuals listed below deserve special recognition for the crucial role they played in this book's development. To each of them, Victoria and I owe an eternity of gratitude.

Readers
Jess M. Brallier and I have been fast friends and publishing colleagues since we started working together at Little, Brown & Company thirty-five years ago. I continue to cherish his friendship, insights, and counsel on a daily basis.

Suzanne Giesemann is a dear friend and author extraordinaire. As a medium and as my spiritual adviser she has given me the ultimate gift: absolute knowledge that my beloved wife, now in spirit form, remains with me 24/7.

Jamie Turndorf is an accomplished author, esteemed radio talk show host, and dear friend who has suffered a grievous loss similar to mine. Her strength, wisdom, and unselfish efforts on my behalf have meant more to me than words can express.

Publishing Team

Mindy Conner of Winston-Salem, NC, has served as my editor for many years. Not only is she best editor of my acquaintance, she is also one of the finest people I have ever known.

Dorie McClelland, president of Spring Book Design. Dorie is the best in the business in designing the interiors of books, and I am blessed to be a recipient of her talent, kindness, and enthusiasm.

Cathy Helms, president of Avalon Graphics. Cathy is the best in the business in creating book covers and book trailers, so again I am blessed to have on my team a professional of style and a friend of quality.

Don Leeper, president of BookMobile. Don is yet another close friend who excels in a commitment to quality print and ebook publishing, as this book confirms. I am indebted to him and his entire staff.

Family and Friends

Here is where it gets hard because so many wonderful people were involved on so many meaningful levels. But I would be thoroughly remiss if I did not highlight here my sister, Clarissa H. Endicott, and her beloved husband, Thomas H. Endicott. Their love and support were central to the publication of this book, in ways I know they understand.

Preface

This book is written for my three sons—Churchill, Brooks, and Harrison—and it chronicles the years from September 1976, when I met Victoria, to May 1984, when our first son was born. During those years that took us from Kansas City to Washington, D.C., to Boston and ultimately to Hingham on Boston's South Shore, Victoria and I found a love that goes far beyond the clichéd "wedded bliss." I truly believe that the love we continue to share is as rare as it is all-consuming, especially in this era in which marriage and other time-honored traditions are under attack. In the heart of the book, therefore, I attempt to explain—from my perspective and I believe from Victoria's—why our marriage was/is so successful and meaningful—and eternal.

I have written this book for four reasons:

First, I want to offer insights to my sons about their mother that they would otherwise not have. As is true of most parents, Victoria and I rarely discussed the years of our dating and early marriage with our children, although we discussed them often between ourselves. I now have the opportunity to do that.

Second, I want to offer those same insights to my sons' children as yet unborn. Without this book as a basis, their children would not have as complete a picture of what an extraordinary person their grandmother was/is, especially after I am gone.

Third, I want to offer these same insights to people who never knew Victoria so that they can understand why her presence on Earth was and continues to be a gift even to those who never met her.

Fourth, when Victoria died of cancer on May 1, 2011, a part of me died with her. At the same time, a part of her lives on in me. As her husband I have the duty, honor, and privilege to keep her memory and spirit alive.

Two footnotes before I begin our story:

Although Victoria's family and childhood friends continue to refer to my wife as "Vicki" (as I did when I first knew her), I use the name "Victoria" in this book because that was her stated preference.

I often use the present tense when describing my wife and our relationship even though she passed on several years ago. I do this because I continue to believe—more and more as time goes by—that Victoria is with me in spirit every hour of every day. *Why* I am so convinced of this is the subject of another book; just know for the purposes of *this* book that I had a coauthor to help me write it.

Chapter 1

I met Victoria Karel on Labor Day 1976. We attended a beach party with a group of friends at Lake Jacomo in Jackson County, Missouri (hence the name of the man-made lake), about an hour's drive east of Kansas City, where everyone in the close-knit party of ten lived. She was someone else's date, a fellow named Peter. I had brought a lady friend named Sue Sheila who worked at Trilogy Bookstore in Kansas City. Everyone attending the party, except for Peter, worked in some literary capacity in Kansas City—for a bookstore, in the book review section of the *Kansas City Star*, in a library, and so on. I was a sales representative for Little, Brown & Company of Boston, and Victoria was serving as an architectural researcher for the local office of the Landmarks Commission. At the time, she was researching the boyhood home of Walt Disney for inclusion on the National Registry of Historic Places. Her work took her often to the downtown branch of the Kansas City Library.

I drove my company car (a very large, dark blue Monte Carlo) to the lake, with Peter and Victoria riding with Sue

Sheila and me. When we neared the lake, we stopped at a 7-11 to pick up some ice, cold drinks, snacks, and whatnot. Peter and Sue Sheila hopped out to make the purchases, leaving Victoria and me alone in the car.

Thinking to make conversation, I turned around and for the first time looked at your mother sitting in the backseat diagonally across from me. Here is where you might expect me to describe rockets going off and choirs breaking out in song. Although that may have been happening, it was not why I was having such a hard time speaking. Nor was it her physical appearance, although she was a strikingly beautiful young woman. It was her radiant smile, pure and simple. It lit up everything around her, including my heart. I don't know how long Peter and Sue Sheila were inside that store, but I distinctly remember wishing they would take their sweet time coming back to the car.

But come back they did, and before Victoria and I were able to say much to each other. We did manage to say a lot to each other after we arrived at the beach, though. Not a lot of personal information, because Victoria was not one to reveal much about herself. About all I was able to garner that afternoon was that she hailed from a town in Nebraska named Howells; she had a brother and two sisters; she had attended the University of Nebraska at Lincoln, where she was a member of Alpha Delta Pi sorority; she had graduated with a BFA degree from the Kansas City Art Institute, one of the premier schools of art in the country, with specializations in painting and printmaking; and she was currently employed by the Landmarks Commission.

To say I was smitten would be an egregious understatement. For me, she was the only person there and the only reason to be there, and I had the distinct impression that she was experiencing the same emotions. So did Peter. On the drive back to Kansas City he made certain that he and Victoria rode in another car.

During the next several days I tried to figure out a way to see Victoria again. I could have just called her, but being an old-fashioned sort of guy, I was sensitive to the fact that she had been someone else's date. Fortunately, I had a close friend my age named Mike McEvers. Mike had attended the beach party and knew everyone who worked in literary circles in Kansas City. As one of the three owners of Trilogy Bookstore he was in effect Sue Sheila's boss—although he never considered himself "boss" of anything. He was a great guy. So I gave Mike a call and asked him if he could help me out. He seemed not at all surprised by my request and told me not to worry, he'd set something up.

True to his word, two days later Mike called to ask me if I could join a group of people for lunch the following Friday at Suzie's, a popular and inexpensive Mexican restaurant in midtown Kansas City. Although I was beginning a heavy fall travel schedule, I quickly agreed and asked, perhaps too casually, "Will Vicki be there?"

"I wouldn't be at all surprised," Mike chortled.

When I arrived at Suzie's that Friday I had no trouble locating my party: seven people I knew were seated at a table set for eight. The lone empty chair was on Victoria's right.

It was a fun lunch, and time sped by. Suddenly Mike jumped to his feet, glanced at his watch, and exclaimed, "My Lord, look at the time. I've got to get back to work!"

Immediately five other people stood up, threw some money on the table, and ran out of the restaurant, leaving Victoria and me sitting there, temporarily speechless.

"Did you set this up?" she asked me at length.

"Well, maybe a little," I confessed. "I asked Mike for help getting us together, but I never expected anything like this. Did *you* have anything to do with it?"

"Well, maybe a little," she confessed with that glowing smile. "But I also think we have some very good friends in common."

I could not disagree.

After we gathered up the money on the table—enough to cover the entire tab plus a handsome tip for our waitress— we consulted our schedules to find a day for our first date. I would be traveling almost constantly through October, and Victoria had several weekend engagements during that same period. We settled on October 30, a date that was to become very meaningful to us in the years ahead.

⌒⌒

This is an appropriate spot to briefly tell you about my own state of affairs at that time, because it has a direct bearing on those early days with your mother.

When I arrived in Kansas City in January 1975 at the age of twenty-seven, I was warmly greeted and quickly accepted by the young crowd who worked within the broad publishing industry there. Many of these individuals were young women. My popularity, such as it was, was based in part on my outgoing personality. But in truth, the greater part of it was based on my perceived "image." I was from

Boston; I worked for one of the world's most prestigious book-publishing companies; and I drove a company car and had a seemingly unlimited expense account. (As I will disclose later, it was by no means unlimited, but it was certainly comprehensive.) What's more, I lived on Warwick Avenue at Inglenook Apartments, a preferred complex adjacent to the tony Country Club Plaza. Suffice it to say that I did not suffer from a lack of female attention. I had a number of male friends too, so my social life on the weekends—and during the week when I was not on the road—was demanding. In short, I was living a life that many people would consider a bachelor's dream.

That began to change a year and a half later when I met your mother on the way to Lake Jacomo—and she was someone else's date. And it changed completely after that lunch at Suzie's—even before our first date. From that day forward I have had no romantic interest in any other woman, and I never will again.

⌒౨

October 30 finally arrived. At six-thirty I drove to Victoria's apartment in an attractive older building on Wyoming Avenue, a thoroughfare near Country Club Plaza and about a ten-minute drive from Inglenook. Because I wanted to make a good first impression, and because I figured we had earned considerable "interest" for lost time in getting to our first date, I took Victoria to Le Mediterranée, a swanky French restaurant located in the heart of the Plaza. I don't remember what she had—I believe it was a veal dish—but I do remember her surprise when I ordered steak tartare.

That someone would eat raw meat was a novelty to her. But being the good sport that she was, she tried a healthy portion and pronounced it "quite good." I have often wondered what role the bottle of French cabernet we ordered played in that comment.

After dinner we went to see the recently released movie *Marathon Man*, starring Dustin Hoffman, and from there to a nightclub for another round of drinks. Every minute of the seven hours Victoria and I spent together that evening was precious to me. People often use the phrase "a magical evening" to talk about a really good date, but "magical" doesn't even begin to describe our first evening together. Long before I said goodnight to Victoria, sometime after midnight, I realized that what I had sensed earlier was real: something novel and profound was indeed happening to me, and it had the potential to forever change my life. I had trouble sleeping that night, restless for the next day and our next date. We had planned an eleven o'clock rendezvous at Frank Theis Park, where we were to play a game or two of tennis before enjoying the first of what was to become a ritual in our life together. How your mother loved picnics!

The life of a book publisher's representative was sometimes extremely busy and sometimes quite laid back. After the first of November there was not much for a book salesman to do other than check stock in major retail and wholesale accounts and catch up on paperwork. By Thanksgiving, all of my accounts had ordered their vital Christmas stock (bookstores make essentially all of their annual profit during the six weeks prior to Christmas). So for three weeks I was in Kansas City every day without a lot to do beyond volunteering as a "floor clerk"—meaning I greeted customers and recommended books when asked to—at Bennett Schneider, the flagship bookstore in Kansas City and one of the finest bookstores of my acquaintance anywhere. Both the buyer and assistant buyer had become my close friends.

The point, of course, is that during this same period Victoria and I had an extended opportunity to spend time together and get to know one another in greater depth. I didn't see her every day—she was working full time and had business obligations—but I did have the joy of seeing her most days throughout the month of November and into December, before I was to leave for a sales conference in Boston followed by Christmas with my parents in Florida.

One way we came to know each other was through the company of others. Victoria cut quite a swath in Kansas City and was often invited to parties. Because she was invited I was invited, and we blended well into the wide overlap of each other's social circles. I enjoyed everyone's company, but what I enjoyed most were the hours I spent alone with your mother. She had been living in Kansas City for several years, and there was much she wanted to show me. In addition to the obvious museums and parks, we attended one of the last games the Scouts played in Kansas City before they moved to Denver to become the Avalanche. We also attended a Chiefs' game, our fifty-yard-line seats compliments of Bennett Schneider Bookstore. Victoria loved going to sporting events, and I think she had a secret crush on George Brett,

the third baseman for the Royals. Then again, so did most
other females in Kansas City.

But our preferred pastime was eating out, especially if the
meal involved breakfast foods or seafood. Being from New
England, I love virtually all seafood, especially shellfish, and
I was delighted to learn that Victoria did too. Salmon was
her favorite, followed closely by swordfish, cod, grouper,
and, eventually, walleye. But it was not so much the food
we savored. It was the setting that allowed us to sit and talk,
often for hours at a time, about everything and anything.
In the thirty-five years I knew your mother, I cannot recall
a single occasion when conversation did not flow fluidly
between us like an endless course of tides. Also, sitting
across from her in a restaurant allowed me to look at her,
always my favorite activity.

One Saturday morning in late November we held a
contest to see who could make the best omelet. The contest
had but one rule: we could use only everyday ingredients as
fillers. The stakes were high, because the loser had to treat
the winner to brunch the following morning at Plaza III, an
upscale restaurant in the Plaza that served the best eggs
Benedict I have ever tasted. I had long prided myself on my
omelet-making ability, and I had noticed during our various outings that Victoria had a strong inclination toward
vegetable omelets. So I went out and bought the freshest
vegetables I could find plus some expensive ham and Swiss
cheese—which I shredded into little bits to sprinkle on top
of the vegetables and on top of the omelet, and thus create
a culinary masterpiece.

On Saturday morning I lit a blazing fire in the hearth and

assembled my ingredients, certain of victory. Victoria arrived promptly at ten o'clock, and we headed to the kitchen for the Big Cook-Off. When she started to remove her ingredients from a paper bag, I became suspicious. "What's in there?" I asked when she placed a small, clear plastic container on the counter. The contents appeared to be delicate pieces of a pure white meat.

"That? Lobster."

"*Lobster?* What did you do? Buy a lobster, cook it, and slice up the meat?"

"Yes," she said, as though that were the most natural thing to do in Kansas City in 1976.

"And in there?" I asked again after she placed another plastic container on the counter.

"Crabmeat."

"Now, just a minute," I groused. "I thought we agreed only to use everyday ingredients."

"These are everyday ingredients, for me," she insisted. "So are these clams, mussels, and scallops," she added as three more small plastic containers emerged from her bag, along with an exquisitely mild Italian cheese, the name of which I could not pronounce, let alone remember.

I was done and I knew it. But it was worth it. Her omelet was the best I have ever tasted. And I didn't mind paying the tab at Plaza III the next morning. It was a memorable start to yet another memorable day. Besides, she had no doubt invested far more money in her "everyday" ingredients than I did on brunch.

⌒つ

Two Saturday evenings later—on what was to be my last full weekend in Kansas City before flying to Boston—I reserved a table at a restaurant on the top floor of a downtown skyscraper that offered magnificent views of the city in all directions. The restaurant also featured ballroom dancing. Victoria loved to dance, and she was much better at it than I was. I didn't mind being second best, though. I got to hold her close when the tempo was slow—and that was sheer joy for me.

It was an enchanted evening—so enchanted that during an orchestral break we continued slow dancing long after the music had stopped. That realization suddenly struck home when I opened my eyes and peered around the dance floor.

"I think we're alone up here," I whispered into Victoria's ear.

"Good," she whispered back. "That's exactly how I like it."

"Me too. But that's not what I mean. I mean, we're *alone* up here. The music has stopped and everyone else has sat down."

"Oh."

Reluctantly we drew apart. As we slowly walked back to our table hand in hand, we were greeted by rousing applause, with many patrons rising to their feet to give us a standing ovation.

"This round is on the house," our waitress exclaimed a few minutes later as she placed two glasses of a rich Bordeaux before us. Victoria and I could only return her smile, and then smile at each other.

◡◦

The Saturday of my departure inevitably arrived, and it was a sad leave-taking. The evening before, Victoria had prepared a Christmas dinner for me at her apartment: roast goose with an assortment of trimmings that any proper Englishman would have found delectable. We tried to make merry, and we succeeded in part, but the pending separation was taking its toll on us. For five weeks now we had been "an item," as you boys would say, although I never regarded Victoria as an "item" in any sense of the word.

During dinner we made plans to stay in touch during the coming three weeks. I would be at a sales conference in Boston for nearly a week, after which I planned to travel to Hancock Point, Maine, to visit my uncle Lansing, and then to Manchester, Massachusetts, to stay for several days with my sister Cris and her husband, Tom, before flying to the Florida Keys to be with my parents for Christmas. Because I would be a moving target before flying south, I suggested to Victoria that if she were to write me a letter, she should send it to Islamorada in care of my parents. I also gave her the key to my apartment in case she wanted to retreat there and enjoy sitting by the fire. I had brought in plenty of chopped wood and had laid a fire in the hearth for her.

The next morning, as she drove me to the airport in her pale yellow 1974 Karmann Ghia (one of the last of its breed made by Volkswagen), we talked about the New Year's Eve party we would be attending after I returned and the plans we had made for January, which included a weekend in Howells to visit her parents. Although I had yet to meet her father, I had met her mother in November during a lunch at Plaza III. She had flown in from Las Vegas, where, she informed us, she had won a carload of cash compliments of a one-armed bandit. What a lady!

When the plane landed in Boston late on Saturday afternoon, I took a cab to the Copley Plaza Hotel, where all twelve sales reps would be staying and where the sales conference was to be held. I checked in, had a bite to eat with the San Francisco rep, who also had arrived early, and then strolled around an area that was, is, and always will be home to me. When I returned to the hotel, acting on a hunch—more accurately, a prayer—I called my apartment. I let the phone ring twice, hung up, and punched in the numbers again: our prearranged signal to confirm that I was the one calling. Victoria picked up on the first ring. You can imagine how happy I was that she did.

The sales conference was uneventful until the final day. At breakfast an administrative assistant told me that the sales manager wanted to see me in his office at 34 Beacon Street at the end of the day. When I reported at the appointed time of four-thirty, I was informed that the New York representative (who was the father of the general manager) had announced his retirement come May, the end of the spring selling season. The position of New York rep had been offered to the current Washington, D.C., rep, but it was unclear if Sandor would accept the offer. He was happily settled where he was—and who wouldn't be—in the genteel confines of northern Virginia. While New York City was and is by far the most lucrative sales territory for every book publisher, and thus for any sales rep, Washington was the most attractive because it included not only the District but also Maryland, Virginia, North Carolina, and Nashville,

Tennessee, site of the headquarters of Ingram Book Company, the largest book wholesaler in the United States to the retail trade. If it turned out that Sandor did refuse the promotion, the sales manager told me, I would be offered New York.

Make no mistake: I love New York. I had spent a lot of time there in my youth and knew the city quite well. But the prospect of being the all-important New York rep after serving only two years in the field in the Midwest was daunting and not a little intimidating. I felt I had no choice, however. My father had often told me that if a company offers you a promotion and you refuse it, you will never receive a second offer. And of course my father was right. He usually was.

So I told the sales manager that I would gratefully accept either offer. And I breathed a sigh of relief the next day when the sales manager telephoned me to say that Sandor and his wife, Phoebe, would be moving to Dobbs Ferry, New York, in May. I would be moving from Kansas City to Washington, a city I had long admired.

Washington, D.C., was a vital book town. Not only were there many popular retail stores in and around the District, the city was high on the list of every book publicist, including those in the New York office of Little, Brown. Most of the company's key authors came through on promotional tours, and I would get to have lunch or dinner with a number of them. Several lived in the Georgetown area, including Herman Wouk and Henry Kissinger. Living and working in D.C. was going to be exciting, and I was thrilled at the prospect.

Nonetheless, other factors weighed heavily on my mind. That evening I called Victoria from Manchester and told her about the promotion. She paused before answering, and when she did, I heard both resolution and sadness in her voice.

"I'm so happy for you, Bill," she said softly. "I shall always wish the very best for you in life."

Right then I wanted to tell her that I had already found the very best for me in life, but I didn't. A telephone conversation is not the best venue to declare that sort of emotion. What I said was, "Let's not talk about this now. Let's wait until I return to Kansas City. I've made reservations at the American Restaurant for seven o'clock that first Saturday evening. We'll talk about it then, but not before, even on New Year's Eve. Deal?"

"Deal," she said. But I could tell her heart was not in it.

I always looked forward to visiting my parents. I could count on good food, good conversation, good vodka, and an adventure or two in the offing. Christmas of 1976 in Islamorada was no exception. Twice, Pappy and I went fishing for bonefish and tarpon in what Keys residents refer to as "the back country," an area on the Gulf side of the Keys of crystalline waters and small, uninhabited islets. We had some luck both times, and my mother celebrated our good fortune—and my promotion—with yet another seafood feast extraordinaire. And there was more. Living in the same complex of Coral Cove were friends who owned a thirty-foot Pearson sloop, and they invited me out for a

day's sail northward toward Key Largo. So there was a lot to
see and enjoy above and beyond Christmas Day, which, as
always with my parents, was a day to remember.

But my heart was elsewhere. While I appreciated everyone's efforts on my behalf, I did not enjoy these outings
with my usual enthusiasm. My parents knew something
was up, not because of my mood, which remained upbeat,
but because nine letters from Victoria were waiting for
me when I arrived—which helps explain why my mood
remained upbeat. When pressed, I simply told them that I
had met an exceptional young woman in Kansas City and
I suspected that they would be hearing more about her in
the near future. They let it go at that. Although my mother
was sympathetic, and I did confide in her a little during our
daily walk together, I said nothing more to my father. It was
usually best to let sleeping dogs lie when it came to Dad
and matters of the heart. A retired investment banker, Dad
tended to put things either in the asset column or the debit
column, with precious little in between. He was frequently
right, but when he was wrong, he could be wrong on a
grand scale. So with him I thought it best to keep my own
counsel until whatever ship was sailing on the horizon came
into clearer focus.

On the morning of December 30 Dad drove me to the
Miami airport. A few hours later my plane landed in Kansas
City, and a few minutes after that Victoria met me halfway
down the jetway. (Back then there was no airport security,
and passengers could come and go pretty much as they
pleased.) Dear Lord, it felt good to be back in her arms
again! I remember that moment as though it happened

yesterday. But the hours between that day and the following Saturday remain largely a blur. I remember trying to keep myself busy planning the next selling season (my last as the Kansas City rep), and of course Victoria and I enjoyed a grand New Year's Eve party at the apartment of her friend (and future bridesmaid) Jody Maugham. But as loving and gracious and kind as your mother always was, a strain had come between us. It was as if she were afraid to get *too* close, to be *too* loving.

Saturday evening came at last. I picked up Victoria at six-thirty and we drove to the American Restaurant, one of our favorite restaurants ever. It was located downtown within the Westin Hotel at Crown Center, an eighty-acre complex that serves as the world headquarters of Hallmark Cards.

When we entered the spacious lobby of the hotel and began walking toward the elevators, I paused and confessed, "I told you a white lie. Our reservation is for seven-thirty, not seven."

When she cocked her head in question, I suggested that we sit by the waterfall and talk for a few minutes. She agreed, and we walked over to what was by anyone's standards a romantic setting. Water splashed from high above into a lagoon-like basin enclosed by a low semicircular wall of smooth, flat marble that served as comfortable seating. A panoply of ferns, greenery, and flowers growing in beds adjacent to the wall scented the air. Incredibly (well, perhaps not so incredibly), there was no one else there. We had the whole nook to ourselves.

After we sat down, we gazed deep into each other's eyes for a few moments—or perhaps it was for a few minutes.

Often when I was with your mother, time seemed to take on a different dimension. At length I took her right hand in both of mine.

"You know I love you, don't you," I said, not as a question. She nodded.

"And that I would do anything in the world for you." Again she nodded.

"And you feel the same about me?"

She nodded a third time, more emphatically.

I raised her hand to my lips, kissed it, and then pressed it to my heart. "Will you marry me, then?"

She nodded a final time, but that was not what sent my heart soaring. It was that smile, the answer I had prayed for.

I took her in my arms and held her close. "I will make you the happiest woman ever to have lived," I murmured into her ear.

"And I will make you the happiest man," she whispered back.

I released my grip and again gazed into her greenish-brown eyes, now welling with tears. "You just did," I said.

Chapter 2

Yes, I know. I proposed to a woman I had known for only a few months. Although this is not necessarily something I would encourage you boys to do, in my case I *knew*. I can't explain how I knew; I just did. I could have proposed to your mother at Suzie's Mexican restaurant on that September day, so sure was I of my heart.

That being said, I do not believe in love at first sight, at least not in the way it is described in fairytales. I realize that may sound incongruous given what I have written thus far, but really it's not. On the day I married your mother, when I saw that beautiful woman walking down the aisle toward me on the arm of her father and her eyes locked on mine, I would have sworn on everything that is holy that I could not ever love her more than I did at that moment. I was convinced beyond any doubt that my love had expanded to its very limits. But I was wrong. And that's the magic of it. There *are* no limits. What I have learned since meeting your mother—what I am still learning from her today, years after she has passed on—is that truly loving another human being is a process that never ends. Because love never ends. Love never dies.

What I do believe can happen—because it most definitely happened to us—is that two people can experience an immediate connection to each other that transcends physical attraction. Some people refer to this phenomenon as "chemistry" or "infatuation" (or "puppy love" for youngsters), and I suppose those labels are as good as any. But whatever it is called, this phenomenon resonates not only with the body, but with the mind and spirit as well. In any meaningful long-term relationship these three core elements act in concert with each other. And because they are inexorably linked together, they cannot be separated or one of them ignored. When they act in synchrony they become the sod, seeds, and April showers that allow love to take root and bloom in a garden that is as fertile as it is infinite.

$\smile$

After the first waves of euphoria washed over us, Victoria and I had some serious planning to do. First item on the agenda: pick a date for the wedding. We needed to inform our families of our intentions, of course, but it seemed prudent to have a date in mind when we did. Since we both love the month of September, we settled on Saturday, the twenty-fourth. That would give us time to organize logistics and me time to have a full selling season in the D.C. territory under my belt. Victoria would continue to work for the Landmarks Commission in Kansas City until several weeks before the wedding, which would take place in Kansas City.

The next question was where the wedding would be held.

Victoria was raised Catholic (and had attended a Catholic elementary school in Howells) and I, Episcopalian. Neither of us touted one sect over the other, or one religious belief over another, because we believed that God doesn't put stock in such things. We are all One with God, regardless. (That statement does not deny the divinity of Jesus Christ, which we always believed in, and I continue to do.) As a historian, I don't see a lot of meaningful difference between Catholicism and Anglicanism, especially when you consider that what first stirred King Henry VIII to break heavenly ties with Rome was his very earthly lust for Anne Boleyn.

During the course of our courtship Victoria and I had attended a number of churches in the city, and the one we were most drawn to was the Country Club Christian Church, an inspiring and open-minded church located on Ward Parkway that welcomed believers of all faiths. We also liked and respected the senior minister, Rev. Tom Lieurance, a kind and gentle man of deep convictions, much like our dear friend Graham Fenton at St. Stephen's Church in Edina. We wanted Dr. Lieurance to marry us, and I was amenable to having a Catholic priest also preside at the service if doing so would be meaningful to Victoria's family. But when we met with a Catholic priest whom we knew to discuss the matter, we discovered that some things hadn't changed much in the Catholic Church since the days of the Inquisition. When the priest, who at first came across as a devout and decent man, abruptly changed tack and informed us in no uncertain terms that he would participate in the ceremony only if we pledged a sacred oath that any children born to us would be raised as good Catholics, we

were taken aback. When I replied straight-faced that my
fiancée and I could not agree to such a condition because
we had already promised a rabbi that we would raise our
children as good Jews, the meeting was over. On the way
back to the car I had to hold Victoria up, fearful that she
might fall down because she was laughing so hard.

During the weekend trip to Howells in late January we
told Victoria's parents the big news. Her mother already
knew—not because Victoria had confided in her, but
because mothers by nature have a keen sense for such
things. Her father, as kind and loving a parent as ever there
was, seemed surprised by the suddenness of the announcement (who can blame him?), but he soon came around. His
beloved Kissinki (which translates from the Czech into
"little kiss," his pet name for Victoria) was clearly so very
happy, and he would not gainsay her happiness.

As a side note, my good relationship with Granddaddy
in the first year or two was based largely on Victoria's
happiness. But before long we drew close to each other for
different reasons, and I started calling him "Dad" because
I wanted to, and he started calling me "William" because
no one else did. It was a name used solely by him. That by
itself is a fond memory.

Telling my parents was a bit more complicated because it
had to be done by phone. My mother also knew what was
up, for the same reasons that Victoria's mother did, and I
suspect that she had advised my father to expect the call.
The first thing Dad wanted to know, of course, was if I had
completely lost my mind. (That was not the first time he
had questioned my sanity.) And if not, had I thought every-

thing through, because this was all rather sudden. Did I really know what I was doing?

"No, Dad, I haven't thought everything through," I replied. "But yes, I do know what I am doing."

When we hung up a few minutes later, I sensed that I had not entirely convinced my father that marriage should be part of my five-year business plan at this point in my life. But I knew Victoria would put his mind to rest once he had occasion to meet her, which would happen, we had agreed, during a trip to Maine over the Fourth of July weekend. Until then I knew I had my mother's support, and that was key. However demure and genteel she might have appeared on the surface, my mother possessed a tenacity and constancy that even General Patton would have admired. (In fact his son, George S. Patton III, *did* admire those traits in your grandmother. He lived in Hamilton, not far from Manchester, and kept his magnificent schooner, the *If and When*, anchored a stone's throw from our house.)

⌒⌒

The days flew by. In what seemed an impossibly short amount of time it was early May and I was packing up the car and driving east toward Washington. The plan was for me to stay at the Chain Bridge Marriott Hotel in McLean, Virginia— across the Potomac River from the District—for approximately a month. During that time I would be working with Sandor and meeting key accounts in the area before I kicked off the official fall selling season in early June.

I would also be looking for a place to live, a search that of course included Victoria. When she flew out for five days during the Memorial Day weekend we scoured the area for a conveniently located and reasonably priced apartment, a far less daunting challenge back then than it is today. We also visited with Victoria's aunt and uncle who lived in Springfield, a Virginia suburb of Washington, and my aunt and uncle who lived in the northwest quadrant of Washington.

In fairly short order we settled on an apartment on Provincial Drive in McLean, not far from the mega shopping center known as Tyson's Corner Center. (That center now incorporates two back-to-back mega malls: Tyson's I and Tyson's II.) It was a lovely apartment: two bedrooms, an area for a study/ home office, a good-sized kitchen, and a large living/dining area. It was perfect for us, and signing the lease was exciting. It made everything seem so blessedly real.

The last day before Victoria was to fly back to Kansas City and I was to get down to serious work, I took Victoria for a drive down Dolly Madison Boulevard toward the Potomac and an area of McLean where rich people live. When she asked me where we were going, I told her we were on our way to meet a mystery friend. The suspense mounted when I drove through an open gateway and past an empty guardhouse onto a long, winding driveway, finally pulling to a stop before a most impressive white mansion surrounded by impeccably manicured lawns and gardens.

Victoria's eyes widened. "What is this place?" she asked reverently, her gaze absorbing the majesty of it all.

"Hickory Hill," I told her.

"Who lives here?"

"Robert Kennedy."

Her jaw dropped. "*Robert Kennedy* lives here?" she asked incredulously.

"Sure," I replied as casually as I could manage. "With Ethel and a big brood of children. Would you like to meet them?"

"You *know* them?"

"No," I said, as I put the car in gear and got the hell out of there.

Here's the point: before I met your mother I could not have dreamed of doing such a thing. It would have been so utterly out of character that no one who knew me would have believed it. But when I was with your mother, anything and everything was possible.

We faced another four-week separation before I would see Victoria in early July. But this time it was different. This time we were formally engaged to be married, and that meant that everything I saw and experienced during the summer months I would be seeing and experiencing with my bride in the fall. Still, I missed her terribly, and most evenings we either called or wrote each other. (Yes, back then, before e-mail and texting, people actually wrote and mailed letters to each other!) On average we exchanged four or five letters a week. The length of a letter didn't matter. What mattered to me was opening an envelope with Victoria's impeccably neat handwriting on it and reading the words of love enclosed inside.

I still recall my first trip to Nashville in June to sell the fall publishing list to the Ingram Book Company. Most publishers release their big titles in the fall to capitalize on the all-important Christmas retail selling season. This year was no exception. Ingram accounted for approximately 20 percent of my employer's annual revenues, so there was no room for mistakes. Little, Brown had a strong publishing list, as it always did, but I was nevertheless nervous. The fact that my boss, the sales manager, would be joining me on this occasion did not help matters. Within any corporation, blame for a screw-up or oversight tends to travel down the chain of command, not up.

After my plane landed at the airport, I picked up a rental car and drove downtown to the Sheraton Hotel. Most publishers and publishers' reps stayed at the Sheraton because it was located near Printer's Alley, a picturesque area of trendy restaurants and bars mixed in with some rather seedy entertainment—if one were so inclined, which I was not. The names "Chesty Morgan" and "Heaven Lee" flashed in neon lights outside one such establishment every time I walked down Printer's Alley. I sometimes wonder if they still do, *in memoriam* if not *in situ*.

I had a couple of hours to wait for the sales manager to arrive, so I decided to go to my room to relax for a while. A few minutes later there came a knock on my door. When I opened it, my jaw dropped. A bellhop was holding a beautifully wrapped cheese tray and a bottle of our favorite Bordeaux. Attached to the multicolored foil surrounding the cheese was a note that read simply: "Good luck. All my love, Vicki."

It was all the inspiration I needed.

I still have that card in a treasure trove of memorabilia.

I took a week's vacation over the Fourth of July weekend (one of the few times of the year when American business virtually shuts down) and flew to Boston to meet Victoria. Before driving to Maine, we stayed in Manchester for a couple of days with my sister Cris and her husband, Tom. Cris and Victoria hit it off immediately, which was a blessing for Victoria because I knew she was anxious about this trip. Not only was it nerve-racking to "meet the parents" (as it was for me in Howells), it was also, in a way, a clash of cultures. Victoria hailed from the great plains of Nebraska, and here she was on Cape Ann, Massachusetts, soon to depart for Hancock Point, Maine. That she had been a camp counselor at Lake Sebago in Maine during two summers and had traveled extensively in New England as a result didn't matter. She was nervous, and I understood why. Meeting my father sometimes made *me* nervous.

So it was with considerable relief that we received an unusually warm reception in Maine. Later I found out why. The previous evening Cris had softened the beachhead by calling our parents. "Believe me, Mirr and Dad," she had gushed into the phone (so my mother told me), "you are *really* going to like her. Tom and I are so impressed!" What a wonderful introduction. The 1st Marine Division could not have done a better job on that beach. God bless you, Colonel Cris.

We did all the things one does in Maine in the summer. We played tennis, went sailing and hiking and canoeing, and enjoyed the bounty of the sea—either at home with my parents, at a restaurant, or at the home of a friend or relative. Slowly Victoria's trepidations began to melt away, as I had been confident they would. For it to work, Victoria simply had to be Victoria. Grace, kindness, and sensitivity on a grand scale go a long way in this world—as I suspect they do in the afterworld.

On the day we left Hancock Point to drive back to Boston, my father gave Victoria a bear hug, something I had rarely seen him give anyone. Dad was simply not a bear hug kind of guy. That more than anything convinced me that the visit had been a smashing success!

I took one more trip out to see Victoria before the wedding. In late August 1977 I flew to Omaha and we drove her Ghia to Howells. There I met for the first time your aunt Mary and uncle Dick Crain and their children, your cousins Kelli and Brian. Kelli was as cute as a buttercup; Brian, well, he was up for anything. If you can believe it, they were both just "knee high to a grasshopper" at the time. We all had a great time together making final plans for the wedding. It was Victoria's and my great joy and privilege to be asked to take Kelli and Brian to the Colfax County Fair, and we had a blast. Such great kids, which was/is no surprise, given who their parents are.

I had been confident.

And then there we were, a week before the wedding. I was planning to leave Washington immediately after a regional sales conference to have two days in Kansas City before the ceremony. All seemed to be in order for what was to be a formal six o'clock wedding at the Country Club Christian

Church, to be followed by a grand reception at the Alameda Hotel in the Plaza.

Then, alas, Nature interfered with Victoria's impeccably laid plans. As the sales conference began in D.C., a terrible storm swept through Kansas City, flooding the Plaza and the first floor of the store in which the bridesmaids' dresses and a number of accoutrements were being stored. What a mess! And I could do nothing to help. But not to worry. With her grit and flair for efficiency Victoria had put everything back in proper order by the evening of the rehearsal dinner at the American Restaurant (where else?).

That dinner of beef Wellington and exquisite wine and champagne was, of course, a memorable event. My father and Uncle Lance ("best men" in every sense of the term) had only nice things to say, and the conversation was lively and happy. My only regret was that Cris and Tom were unable to attend. My other sister, Diana, a nurse who worked in the nation's first hospice center in Connecticut, was able to attend and served as a bridesmaid. Diana had met Victoria for the first time two days before the wedding. I will never forget how she described my bride to me the evening of the rehearsal dinner.

"Never in my life," she said, "have I met someone so gracious, so regal, so kind. Victoria is like a princess. You are so very fortunate."

Amen to that, Di-Di.

⌣⌒

Recounting the wedding would be trying to describe something indescribable. Suffice it to say that every moment of both the wedding and reception are forever etched in my brain and in my heart.

The only hitch came afterward when we embarked in a taxi for the airport. Our plan was to fly first to St. Louis to spend our wedding night at the Cheshire Inn, one of our favorite hostelries. The next day we would fly to Miami, rent a car, and drive to Cheeca Lodge in Islamorada, another favorite of mine—and eventually, ours. On the third day we would fly to St. Croix in the U.S. Virgin Islands to spend six days and five nights at the Caneel Bay Resort on St. John.

We never made it to St. Louis. Our friend, usher, and self-appointed majordomo Mike McEvers put our luggage in the wrong cab! When we arrived at the airport we had no luggage. As disappointing as that was, there was nothing for it but to stay at the Airport Marriott and wait for our luggage to be returned to us. Which it eventually was, in the wee hours of the morning.

And the delay wasn't all bad. The next morning, while waiting for our newly booked flight from Kansas City to Miami, we got to see off my parents and uncle and sister, as well as others in the wedding party, including my lifelong friend Joe Cheshire. All's well that ends well, as the great bard used to say. And as Victoria used to say, there's usually a silver lining in any adversity if you have the patience to look for it and the wisdom to recognize it.

Chapter 3

I admit to having limited experience with wedding trips, but when it comes time for you boys to book yours, I heartily and without reservation recommend Caneel Bay. What a trip that was!

Caneel Bay Resort, built on land once owned by Laurance Rockefeller, is on the island of St. John in the sun-drenched U.S. Virgin Islands. It is accessible only by boat. Several thousand people live on the island, primarily in two small towns, the larger of which is Cruz Bay. Despite the presence of others on the island, though, and of course at Caneel Bay, Victoria and I had the distinct impression that we *owned* it, both at the resort and especially at our palm-shaded bungalow on Turtle Bay. How the staff managed to instill that sensation is beyond me. That they did has been reason enough to make Caneel Bay a favorite destination of the *crème de la crème* of our global society. Excellence to that degree rarely becomes stale or rusty over time.

Lest you begin to wonder if the name Vanderbilt or Carnegie is part of your pedigree, let me assure you it is not. The only *crème* of which we can boast is what we pour into our morning coffee. Victoria and I were on the "honeymoon special," an arrangement that featured six days and five nights on one of the most beautiful tropical islands on Earth. Included in the package were complimentary (and delectable) buffet breakfasts and dinners orchestrated by a symphony of chefs and waiters holding court under an enormous canopy near the beach; a champagne midnight cruise on a seventy-foot Cris Craft; and a number of other amenities such as use of a Sunfish sailboat at any time. The only out-of-pocket expenses at Caneel were lunch, liquor, souvenirs, and rental Jeeps, were we so inclined—and we were. More on that in a moment.

What did all this cost? Not as much as you might suspect. The tab was $549—not for one night but for the whole enchilada. This was 1977, of course, and prices were lower then. And there was a catch. Late September is in the heart of the hurricane season in the Caribbean, and if for any reason we had to cancel our trip or flee the island, there would be no refund. But we were not worried. Nor, as it turned out, did we have reason to be. Every day on that island we were blessed with chamber of commerce weather. We hardly ever saw a cloud. And on that midnight cruise a nearly full moon cast a romantic glow across the Leeward Islands that could have melted the heart of Satan.

Trying to pick out the highlights of those six unforgettable days is a little like trying to decide whose version of paradise is more appealing. But one incident does stand out.

I learned something about your mother on our first full day at Caneel Bay. She loved Jeeps. Not the kind of Jeep Liberty we own today, but the classic open-air Jeep you see in World War II movies. Victoria took to Jeeps the way some women take to thoroughbred horses and some men take to flashy sports cars—and the way you and I take to sailboats.

So of course we rented one that first day and tooled around the island, "uphill and over dale" as my mother used to say. Because 60 percent of the island of St. John is protected as the Virgin Islands National Park, there was plenty of wild terrain to explore. In that sense it was much like the Ding Darling National Wildlife Refuge on Sanibel Island, as we were to discover in future years.

At one stop, after snapping a few photos, Victoria announced that she was taking command of the Jeep. She knew how to drive a stick shift because her Ghia featured "four on the floor." Besides, back in those days a lot of people learned to drive using a clutch, even though most cars sold at that time had an automatic transmission at least as an option. For many it was standard equipment, and a buyer had to request a standard shift. Still, the philosophy of being tested for a driver's license using a clutch shift makes sense. This same "back to basics approach" is followed today at the Naval Academy. Before a midshipman steps on board a destroyer or aircraft carrier, he or she must first learn the ropes on a sailing vessel.

So Victoria knew what she was doing when, a mile or two down the road, she veered onto a swath of grass, crashed through some low-lying brush, and drove out onto a beach. For a mile or two we cruised along the water's edge as sandpipers, terns, and other shorebirds scurried or took flight to get out of our way.

"Where are we going?" I shouted out over the roar of the engine and whistling wind.

"I'm not sure," she shouted back.

"Looking for anything in particular?"

"Yes. And I'll know it when I see it."

"See what?"

"The most secluded stretch of beach on this island."

That got my attention. I looked askance at her. "Why?" I asked innocently.

"Because tomorrow we're going there for a picnic."

Ultimately, she found her spot. And the next day we returned with two box lunches from Caneel and a bottle of French wine.

It was quite a picnic. One of our best ever.

⌒

The six days passed as though in a dream, and too soon we were on a plane bound for National Airport (now known as Reagan International Airport). The timing was good because we had been in McLean for only two days, sleeping on a mattress on the floor and eating off plastic plates, when Victoria's furniture and Ghia arrived from Kansas City along with several household items Cris had sent us from Manchester.

We still had a number of gaps to fill, and we took our time filling them—not through the convenience of a furniture store but by snooping around estate sales and visiting antique stores. Your mother was a traditionalist in every sense of the word, and purchasing furniture was no exception. To me, a piece of furniture was a piece of furniture.

But not to Victoria. Slowly (because she believed that anything worth doing was best done slowly and deliberately) I found myself not only tolerating our weekend outings but looking forward to them. Antiquing became a lifelong interest for us both, and I learned so much from your mother—about antiquing and about many other pursuits of value.

During the week, of course, I was selling books. The process was the same as in Kansas City, the big difference being that there were so many bookstores in the Washington metro area that I was able to work from our apartment in McLean three out of every four weeks. Only when I was in Nashville or traveling across North Carolina to Blacksburg, Virginia, did I spend nights away from home. The rest of Virginia, and that included Charlottesville, was, for me, within striking distance of Washington. The standard rule of thumb regarding the corporate expense account was that a rep could stay in a motel if he or she were more than fifty miles from home at the end of a business day. Charlottesville was more than twice that, but I gladly drove well into the night to be home with your mother, if only for a few hours before I retraced my route early the next morning. The benefits? I got to sleep next to her and I was saving money for my company!

Although she was hesitant at first, because she wasn't sure it was appropriate, I convinced Victoria during that first season to accompany me on several day trips to Annapolis and parts of the Maryland Eastern Shore. She loved it, of course, because while I sold my accounts she could explore new territory in the full splendor of fall in the Upper South. (I noted on that trip that a good many midshipmen at the Naval Academy also appreciated Victoria's presence on their campus.) Traveling with your mother on these occasions turned the mundane into the sublime. The daily challenge of being a rep was all the driving, either on the open road or in city traffic; but having Victoria beside me and occasionally helping out with the driving turned lemons into lemonade.

Speaking of treats, this is a good opportunity to introduce one of Victoria's great passions: ice cream. When Victoria and I started dating, several of her friends told me that she was so obsessed with ice cream that she carried an ice cream scoop in the glove compartment of her Ghia. I found that hard to believe, so the first time I was a passenger in her car, I flipped open the glove compartment on the pretext of finding a city map for Shawnee Mission, Kansas. And there it was: an old-fashioned metal ice cream scoop.

I pulled it out and held it up.

"What's this for?" I asked her.

She gave it a quick glance. "For when I have an ice cream attack," she said.

"But you'd need a pint or a quart to use one of these."

"Or a gallon," she countered.

"Come on, now, be serious."

"You don't believe me? Here, I'll show you. I just happen to feel an attack coming on."

As Fate would have it, we could see a Baskin-Robbins up the road. She drove into the parking lot, went inside, and came out a minute later with a quart of ice cream, a plastic dish, and two red plastic spoons.

"Want some?" she asked politely. "It's mint chocolate."

"You bet," I said. The day was hot, and a heaping dish of ice cream sure sounded good.

She proceeded to scoop a tiny amount into the dish— approximately enough to satisfy the gastronomic cravings of a field mouse—and handed it to me.

In response to my questioning look, she happily announced, "The rest is for me."

And it was. And she sat there smiling the whole time. At agonizing length I asked, "Are we done yet?"

"Almost," she chirped as she flipped the quart container upside down to capture every last drop of the liquefied delight.

Okay, point taken and lesson learned. You don't mess with Texas and you don't mess with Victoria's love of ice cream.

Over the years friends and colleagues have had serious debates over her favorite flavor. Unpleasant words have been exchanged, and on several occasions fisticuffs nearly broke out. But to me the answer was a no-brainer: jamoca almond fudge. Baskin-Robbins must have been out of it that day we stopped in Shawnee Mission.

⌒

We started a tradition that first fall together in Virginia and continued it every year until you boys were born: we spent Thanksgiving with Victoria's family and Christmas with mine one year, and vice versa the next year. That involved a lot of travel, but Victoria and I loved to travel together. And there were many benefits because both sets of parents treated us like royalty. That first Christmas, in Islamorada, my father formally introduced his daughter-in-law to *his* great passion in life: fishing. Pappy was a master angler, whether it be with heavy tackle, fly rod, spinning rod, or a simple bait-casting rod, and numerous prizes and trophies confirmed his skill. When you were out with him on a charter boat in the Gulf Stream and a big fish struck, you were supposed to know immediately what to do and where to go, whether or not you were the one with the fish on your line. It was no doubt the same sort of drill with the same sort of urgency that sailors practiced during World War II, in case their ship spotted a U-boat—or worse, a torpedo speeding toward them.

As the charter boat's mate instructed Victoria in the intricacies of deep-sea fishing, Captain Dick gunned the boat out of Bud & Mary's Marina. Victoria listened politely to the mate, but I knew she wasn't paying close attention. She didn't have much interest in fishing unless the outing involved a picnic. I was sitting in the starboard aft fighting chair fishing a flat line. Victoria was sitting in the chair directly behind me, her fishing rod placed in a socket beside her and her line clipped to the starboard outrigger. Dad was standing in the middle of it all, surveying the arena of battle, his full attention on the other flat line and port outrigger.

We had had no luck whatsoever, and by mid-afternoon even I was feeling the soporific effects of a warm sun and gentle sea motion. Then, all of a sudden, an enormous sailfish came surging out of the water with Victoria's bally-hoo bait in its mouth. It poised for a moment, its long bill pointing skyward, crashed back into the sea and took off on a wild run as Victoria's line screamed off its reel.

From my many years in boot camp training I knew what to do—reel in the other lines as quickly as possible and get the rods out of the way of the fisherman—and I did that with the flat lines while the mate started reeling in the port outrigger line. That left Victoria pretty much to her own devices for the moment, and clearly she was at sea. I glanced over at her as I reeled like crazy and she gave me a "What in God's sweet name do I do *now?*" look. Dad, bless him, was there to help his daughter-in-law. Shortly after the initial onslaught that had everybody hopping, he switched from his customary role of Captain Bligh on the quarterdeck to one more in keeping with Mahatma Gandhi on a peace march. He shouted encouragement to Victoria and took the other outrigger rod from the mate so the mate could assist Victoria. All the mate did, I swear, was transfer the butt of the rod from its holder into the socket on the front end of her fighting chair. Her line, meanwhile, continued to scream in protest, and by now there wasn't much of it left on the spool.

"Strike him!" the mate cried out.

"*Strike him?*" Victoria shouted back. "*How?*"

"Hit the drag lever"—he pointed to the mechanism on the side of the reel—"and when you feel the full weight of the fish on the line, pull back on the rod like you mean it. You need to set the hook."

I can't imagine what was going through Victoria's mind at that moment—although I had a keen sense of where she wanted to set that hook—but she did as she was told. Again the nearly seven-foot sailfish leapt into the air, shaking its head and seemingly walking on its forked tail on the sea for several moments before falling back. This went on for a good thirty minutes. Victoria was approaching her limit of endurance—as was the fish. Finally, after another grueling fifteen minutes, the mate grabbed the leader, making it an official catch. It had been a magnificent fight, and I could tell that Victoria was both pleased and proud—although Victoria being Victoria, she pooh-poohed her accomplishment whenever the subject came up in future years.

After the sailfish was tagged and released, my father paid your mother the ultimate compliment—the equivalent of a prince of England knighting a hero on the field of battle. He walked solemnly across the deck to where she was sitting, looked her straight in the eye, and shook her hand, one fisherman to another.

Now you boys know the full story of the legendary Big Fish that your mother caught off Islamorada that Christmas, a saga that was written up in both the *Howells Journal* and the *Miami Herald*.

⌒

For Christmas that year Victoria and I bought each other some camping gear on sale at L.L. Bean. The idea was more Victoria's than mine. I knew that in her youth she had been a Campfire Girl—an organization akin to Girl Scouts of America—but I was surprised to learn that she truly liked everything to do with camping. I had done very little of it in my life. Pappy and I had gone camping overnight once or twice in the Ipswich River Wildlife Sanctuary on Cape Ann—as would Victoria and I many years later—but most of my "camping out" had been in the cabin of a boat, not in a tent.

But I was game, as Victoria and I usually were when it came to pursuing the other's interests. During the course of the winter we discussed—often at Aux Fruits de Mer, a fabulous Georgetown eatery that served a superb and surprisingly inexpensive bouillabaisse—when and where we would take our first camping trip. As to when, we settled on the last week in April just before a sales conference in Boston. It was a time when business would be slow. As to where, we picked Shenandoah National Park, located about seventy miles from Washington in Virginia's Blue Ridge Mountains. The park was renowned for its rugged and challenging backcountry, and for the scenic Skyline Drive, a hundred-mile road that runs along the ridge of the mountains. We had never driven it and looked forward to doing so.

If ever you have occasion to spend a spring in the Washington, D.C., area, take full advantage of it. There is nothing quite like springtime in the South, particularly during cherry blossom season (a moving target, but generally mid-March to mid-April). The autumn splendor of New England comes close, but despite my Yankee heritage I have to give the nod to the intoxicating cherry blossoms, azaleas, daffodils, rhododendrons, and dogwoods that explode with color and scents during springtime in the South. For a romantic setting, Paris in April is the stuff of legends. But for my money nothing beats Washington in April.

In late April Victoria and I took off in the Ghia (it's more fun to drive a stick shift in hilly terrain) for Fort Royal, gateway to the Shenandoah Mountains. We had read the park rules and were reminded of them at the welcome center. Among other talking points we were advised to be on alert for bears and poisonous snakes. As it turned out, we did see several bears on our hikes but no snakes—if you discount the two we saw slithering around the welcome center hissing at each other and their kids. We were also reminded that campfires were forbidden anywhere in the backcountry. Aware of this taboo, we had packed several precooked meals along with our tent and sleeping bags. Not the ideal way to camp out, but we had no choice. And we certainly appreciated the reason for the rule.

That Friday evening, as we sat on the ground together outside our tent in what could have been the middle of any vast wilderness, I gazed up at a cloudless and moonless sky. The only light beyond the feeble twinkle of stars was provided by the last wisps of dusk and a kerosene lamp in our tent. All around us, crickets and other creatures of the night had launched into their nightly symphony of pleasing sounds.

"Marvelous, isn't it," I said quietly, truly awestruck.

Victoria followed my gaze. "Yes, it is."

"Makes one ponder cosmic questions."

"Such as God's plan for us?"

I nodded, still staring up. "That, and one even more profound."

"What could that be?"

I looked at her. "What is a Campfire Girl without a campfire?"

She pondered that as she poured out the last of the wine into our plastic cups. "A girl," she said. "And aren't you lucky."

Yes, I was.

Chapter 4

While at a sales conference at the Parker House, which would become our favorite Boston hotel, I received a call from Victoria with some startling news. The owners of the apartment complex where we were living in McLean had decided to convert the apartments into condominiums. Unless we were in the market to buy a condo, which we weren't, we had to vacate the premises by May 31, the end date of our lease.

"Don't worry," I told her. "There are plenty of places to rent. We'll have no trouble finding another apartment."

"Or a house," Victoria said. "I'm already on it."

True to her word, within a week Victoria had found the ideal home for us: a cozy brick Tudor-style house on Bellefonte Avenue on the edge of Old Town, Alexandria. The owner was a U.S. Navy submarine captain who was being posted to the Royal Navy's Faslane Flotilla in Scotland. He and his family would be gone for two years, a time frame that seemed appropriate to us. So we closed the deal, and both parties were pleased with the outcome.

It was hard to leave the apartment in McLean, of course. It had been our first home and we had many happy memories of the year we had spent there; but now we had something even better to look forward to. Such is often the way of life if you remain open to possibilities.

On June 1 we were physically in the house, although there was still a lot of work to do before we could consider ourselves moved in. Victoria saw to that while I set to work selling the all-important fall publishing list, which had as its lead title *American Caesar*, the epic biography of Gen. Douglas MacArthur written by William Manchester, one of my favorite authors. Such was the dream of every book rep: it was never a question of a bookseller buying the title; it was a question of how many copies and making certain that books were evenly distributed. This title was destined to be a number one bestseller on the *Washington Post* and *New York Times* lists—and virtually every other legitimate media outlet nationwide. To be at the epicenter of all the excitement and hype was exhilarating. The cherry on top of the icing on top of the multitiered cake was that Victoria and I got to host a dinner for Mr. Manchester at the five-star 1789 Restaurant—at company expense, of course. It was an evening neither of us would ever forget. He was a gentleman in every sense of the word, from the way he dressed and conducted himself to his kindness in deflecting attention away from himself and onto us. It was as though we were the focus of the evening, and not this internationally renowned author. Victoria was as impressed with him as I was; perhaps even more so.

It was a busy summer, not only selling books but setting

the stage for the entire fall publishing list, which included other important titles in addition to *American Caesar*. In this effort Victoria was a big help. Attending to details is not my forte—I believe my second-grade teacher, Ms. Elizabeth "Hippo" Houseman, was the first to point that out— but it was your mother's. She was a perfectionist bar none, and she gladly took charge of making appointments for me and keeping track of telephone calls from booksellers, publicists from the New York office, and the sales manager in the home office in Boston. Aside from a trip to Nashville, I was not able to do much traveling out of the greater Washington metro area until August. When that time came, I asked Victoria if she would like to travel with me on what would have to be a quick trip through North Carolina and southern Virginia. We had made two trips together that summer to the Maryland Eastern Shore—staying at the Tidewater Inn in Easton on the first, and then at the Robert Morris Inn in Oxford, both outstanding establishments—and those trips had included getaway beach weekends on the coast of Delaware. But that was it; otherwise we had spent the summer in and around the District. So when the time came to visit bookstores in the southern reaches of my territory, I felt that Victoria deserved a break as much as I. Besides, I hated the thought of leaving her for a week.

At first she demurred, thinking that she should be looking for a full-time job. I understood Victoria's position, and I didn't use undue persuasion. I simply told her that it wouldn't hurt if she first traveled with me for ten days, mostly at company expense, through some lovely country. We would start with a weekend on Cape Hatteras and end the following Saturday evening at her favorite hostelry: the Boar's Head Inn in Charlottesville, Virginia, where we would spend the day sitting by the pond sipping mint juleps and watching the swans swim by. That sealed the deal and sent her off to begin making lists of what to bring on the trip—the perfectionist in her again.

You must be wondering about my company expense account because it comes up so often and seems so generous. It was. Essentially, whenever a rep was traveling on company business, the company paid all expenses—within reason, of course. The sales manager reviewed every expense report before signing off on it, and if there were irregularities, there could be hell to pay. That, at least, was the theory, but in reality it was pretty loose. The only criticism I ever received after submitting an expense report was that I was not spending *enough* on entertainment. Virtually anyone involved with selling Little, Brown books was fair game to invite out for lunch or dinner (or a liquid lunch or dinner, as was often the case in publishing in those days), and that included friends. For example, Victoria and I often entertained John Letterman, the book buyer at the Smithsonian, a fellow our age who became a close friend to us both. John was a great guy with but one weakness: he was prone to fall in love with anyone wearing a skirt and looking in his direction. Victoria and I shared more than a few laughs whenever we (more accurately, whenever Little, Brown) treated John and his "flame du jour" at some local eatery. But it was completely justified in the eyes of the company. The bookstore at the Smithsonian invested a lot of money each year in Little, Brown titles, and John Letterman was the Smithsonian's investment adviser, so to speak. John once told me—jokingly, but also with a grain of truth—that Little, Brown's share of the overall Smithsonian portfolio increased every time he so much as glanced at my wife.

⌒

At noon on a Friday in early August we loaded up the Monte Carlo and headed southeast toward the Virginia coast. After passing the Norfolk Naval Base at Hampton Rods—the largest naval station in the world—we headed into North Carolina and the barrier islands that make up the Outer Banks, much of which is a national park. While I was a student at the University of North Carolina at Chapel Hill I had traveled often to these magnificent islands, either with friends or solo, to spend a weekend enjoying the endless beaches. One of my closest friends, Joe Cheshire, had a beach cottage at Nags Head at which I have spent much quality time in my life. But it was the island just south of Hatteras, the most remote island of them all, that I was most looking forward to introducing to Victoria.

Ocracoke Island has a romantic history, and not just because the infamous pirate Blackbeard met his end there in 1718 at the hands of the Royal Navy. One of the first islands on the Atlantic Seaboard to be populated by English settlers, Ocracoke was cut off from the rest of North Carolina for several centuries, and its natives—at least the older ones—speak a unique brand of English. When I first visited the island in the 1960s I heard some islanders use the word "prithee" for "please," and refer to high tide as "hoi toide." To this day, locals are referred to as "high tiders." By the time Victoria and I arrived fifteen years later, Ocracoke was connected to the mainland by three ferries and a private airstrip and had become a popular tourist destination. Sadly, much of that unique Elizabethan brogue had become assimilated into more modern southern dialects.

As I knew she would, Victoria quickly fell in love with Ocracoke's sand dunes, salt marshes, picturesque village, twelve miles of national park seashore, and wild ponies. During that weekend we saw just about everything there is to see, including a cemetery in which are buried the remains of British sailors drowned and washed ashore during World War II after prowling German U-boats torpedoed and sank their ships. It is one of the few places outside the United Kingdom over which the British flag flies 24/7.

During the next year we would visit Ocracoke two more times. For years thereafter Victoria talked about writing a children's book about the island. I wish she had. There was plenty of material for her to choose from, and she could have done the artwork in addition to the writing. It would have been a bestseller.

⌒

The following month, to celebrate our first anniversary, we ventured to a destination that was the diametric opposite of Ocracoke Island. Throwing caution (and our checkbook) to the wind, I made a reservation at the Plaza Hotel in New York City, certainly one of the most fashionable establishments on Fifth Avenue. We drove the Ghia this time, and it was quite something to see Victoria's little yellow Volkswagen parked in front of that palatial building in a line of cars featuring Bentleys, Rolls-Royces, Mercedes, and stretch limousines, as well as horse-drawn carriages for hire. Always the consummate photographer, Victoria whipped out her Nikon and snapped a roll of film of that bizarre sight.

Victoria in New York was like a little girl on Christmas morning. She loved everything about the city: the sights, the delicatessens (Carnegie's was her favorite, but we also frequented Wolf's Sixth Avenue, a pure delight), the bus and boat tours, the night lights, the walks through Central Park, you name it. The highlight came on Saturday evening when we went to see a performance of *42nd Street*, the smash Broadway hit, followed by dinner at the Russian Tea Room. On the walk back to the hotel at midnight we passed by a colorfully dressed South American Indian who had his llama (I'm not making this up) tied to a lamppost. Only in New York!

Late on Sunday afternoon we fired up the Ghia and headed back to Washington. Victoria was sad to leave New York. She had taken only a nibble out of the Big Apple, and she wanted mouthfuls. But I couldn't offer her that. Granted, the Plaza is not the cheapest place to stay in New York, but any hotel worth staying at in the city costs a pretty penny, and we simply couldn't afford such trips on a publisher's rep's salary.

But as it did so often during our marriage, Fate was about to play a kind hand. Little, Brown distributed several lines of books to the retail trade, including Time-Life Books (Time Inc. owned Little, Brown). Because the headquarters of Time-Life Books was in downtown Alexandria, about two miles from our house, I went there frequently to have lunch with the sales manager and/or the publicity director. Your mother sometimes accompanied me on these lunches (always at the insistence of those fellows—she wouldn't have allowed me to mix business with pleasure in such a fashion otherwise), and so it was that two weeks after returning to Washington, Victoria and I joined Nick Benton, the urbane publicity director of Time-Life Books, for lunch at a popular Italian restaurant on King Street.

Until that day I had not known that one of Nick's responsibilities, in addition to promoting his company's books, was managing the Time Inc. suite in New York in the Windsor Hotel on Sixth Avenue (more properly called Avenue of the Americas) directly behind the Plaza. The suite was used to accommodate out-of-town visitors to Time Inc. and included three nicely appointed bedroom suites plus a common living room and dining room and a full kitchen.

This all came to light toward the end of a most agreeable lunch, when Nick casually inquired, "Do you two enjoy going to New York?"

I glanced at Victoria, who, to her eternal credit, remained straight-faced.

"Who doesn't?" I responded.

"Well, then," Nick said, "the next time you're planning to go there over a weekend, give me a call. I'll check the schedule, and if no one is booked to stay there, the suite is yours. We don't normally have guests on the weekends, so it shouldn't be a problem, ever."

"What about other Time and Little, Brown employees?" I asked.

Nick smiled. "They either don't know about the suite or I haven't invited them. No one gets in without my say-so. However," he added on a cautionary note, "there is one condition I must insist upon."

I nodded. "Name it."

"You don't tell anyone about our arrangement."

"We promise," Victoria and I cried out in response.

So it was that a lowly book rep who didn't work for Time-Life Books was able to take his bride to New York on numerous occasions, both from Washington and later from Boston, and stay in a suite fit for presidents and CEOs of multinational corporations. We never paid a dime for lodging and had the luxury of cooking many of our meals in the suite. Only on one occasion in perhaps ten or twelve visits did anyone else stay in the suite while we were there. And we enjoyed the company of that distinguished elderly French couple so much that we all had dinner together one evening—in the suite, with all of us pitching in to create a meal even Escoffier would have admired.

The use of that suite was an incredible gift to us. And I will believe to my last breath that Victoria played a pivotal role in inspiring Nick's generosity. What other explanation can there be?

Whatever your motivation, Saint Nick, thank you.

⌒つ

Winter moved comfortably into spring, and suddenly it was cherry-blossom time in Washington and we were planning a summer vacation to Maine to visit my parents. At the American Booksellers' Convention (now called Book Expo) in Chicago in early June, I received an invitation to dine alone with the sales manager in the Cape Cod Room at the Drake Hotel, where we were staying. Bottom line: I was being offered the position of assistant sales manager.

At first blush it seemed a great opportunity. Boston is my hometown, and the prodigal son would at last be returning. But there was more involved than that. Victoria and I loved living in Washington, and she was pursuing several promising job opportunities—including one at Time-Life Books. Moving to Boston would mean her giving up those possibilities. It would also mean giving up the company car along with a host of other benefits, including my independence. Most ominously, it would mean that I would be going "inside," and that was not necessarily a wise career move at Little, Brown. Someone may write a book someday about why that was so, but it boiled down to the fact that a sales manager at Little, Brown had the life expectancy of a second lieutenant in Vietnam. Although the life expectancy of an assistant sales manager might be a bit longer, the cruel reality was that the natural step up the corporate ladder was from the frying pan into the fire.

I reacted positively to the offer but asked for a little time to consider it and to contemplate such a big change in our lives. I was given two weeks.

When I returned to Washington and told Victoria about the promotion, I could tell right away that she too had reservations—for the same reasons I did. Our reservations, however, became moot after we arrived in Hancock Point and I informed my parents of the offer. The next morning Victoria and I sat down with my father at the rectangular dining table on the front porch that doubled as an ad hoc corporate boardroom conference table. The outcome of our discussion was never in doubt. "Accept the offer or plan to leave the company," was Dad's verdict. I knew he was right—even though the New England rep had years ago turned down such an offer to remain in the field, and he seemed quite content with his decision. I had no desire to leave Little, Brown. I loved the books the company published, and I had (and continue to have) great respect for those employees I worked with. But the die was cast that very afternoon when I called the sales manager to tell him I was accepting the offer and would be in his office the following week to finalize the details.

To this day I question whether I made the right decision. Promotions are usually a good thing, but that job in Washington was certainly one of the best I have ever had—if not *the* best. Of course, I have to add that Victoria and I were newlyweds at the time in one of the most exciting and romantic cities in the world. Or perhaps we just *made* it seem exciting and romantic because we were so much in love with each other and with life itself. Whichever it was, I will forever treasure those glorious days under the Virginia sun.

Chapter 5

At this point you boys are probably thinking, "Jeez, Dad, this all sounds so idyllic. Didn't you and Mom ever *fight?*"

Well, no, we didn't, if by "fight" you mean the "rock 'em, sock 'em" kind of fighting you see in the movies with invective and silverware hurled about the kitchen like broadsides in a naval engagement. That sort of nonsense was simply not in either the Karel or the Hammond gene pool. The mental image of Granddaddy throwing a pan at Grandmommy is as ludicrous as the image of Pappy throwing a pot at Mirr. It never happened—with them or with us.

That is not to say that your mother and I always agreed on everything. We didn't; not by a long shot. We disagreed often. But while many couples in a dispute tend to emphasize what separates them on a particular issue and allow wounds to fester and spread, Victoria and I tried to find common ground that allowed us to build something meaningful on it. The most important consideration was always our relationship, and no argument or difference of opinion was worth damaging that. Our marriage came first; whatever came second was somewhere far back in the distance.

Victoria was no pushover. Don't believe she was for a moment. She could be stubborn and calculating, but always in a gracious and feminine sort of way. In that sense she was much like my own mother, who instinctively knew how to get what she wanted from my father without ever raising her voice or harassing him in any way. My two sisters and I learned early on that if we wanted something from Pappy, we first went to Mirr. If she approved of whatever we were after, we were in like Flynn.

Your mother and I certainly flared up at times—you've seen it happen because those flare-ups were usually directed at one of you—but even when one of us was angry with the other, we could never stay mad. Whatever the root cause of the disagreement might be, in the grand scheme of things it never seemed to matter that much.

Just as it usually is better to seek a compromise than to dig in your heels, it is usually better to make love than war, especially when the conflict involves someone you love more than your own life. Some people claim that the physical joy of making up after a fierce altercation is worth the emotional stress and pain sparked by the argument. To them I say, fine; whatever floats your boat. That perspective would have sunk ours.

Another personal observation, for what it's worth, is that while Victoria and I did disagree on a number of issues—and that is a healthy state of affairs in a marriage—we shared many of the same perspectives on life: in politics, education, religion, food, choice of wine, and just about anything else you can imagine. They say that opposites attract, and undoubtedly that is true for some people. But my strong hunch is that a marriage is less likely to derail if both partners are traveling on the same track toward Grand Central Station. Although Victoria and I came from different backgrounds, we shared many of the same values. In the vast majority of cases she thought as I did, and I thought as she did—until, inevitably, we each became the natural extension of the other in thought, word, and deed. Early in our marriage I ceased referring to myself as "I" except in matters of business. Socially, it was always "we" because I no longer wished to differentiate myself from her in any way.

Okay, back to the story.

The first thing we had to do once we arrived in Boston was find a place to live. Little, Brown was willing to put us up at the Parker House for only so long. We knew we wanted to live in the city, so we looked first on Beacon Hill. Back in 1979, before gentrification, it mattered where you lived on Beacon Hill. There were preferred enclaves, such as Louisburg Square, where the rich and famous lived, and less preferred enclaves, such as Revere Street, where a classmate of mine in elementary school was mugged and left to die. (He didn't, thank God.) We were looking for something in the middle, and we found it on Chestnut Street, a charming area of tree-lined sidewalks and red brick townhomes located just a five-minute walk from the Little, Brown offices on the corner of Joy and Beacon Streets. Trouble was, it had been recently vacated by two doctors, man and wife, who had left the place in shambles. They owned a number of cats, and there was cat poop everywhere, along with a host of other unmentionables. You had to use the full extent of your imagination to "see" this apartment cleaned up and livable, and to ignore the personal hygiene of these two physicians who were practicing at Massachusetts General, one of our nation's finest hospitals.

And there was another problem. When I asked the rental agent if burglaries were a concern, he said, "Yes, but the burglars come in only during the daytime, never at night. And to my knowledge this apartment has not been burglarized for several years." Not the best sales pitch.

Maybe it was the stench of cat poop that had kept would-be burglars at bay, but we didn't want to test that theory. Reluctantly, because the apartment did have great possibilities, we looked elsewhere and ended up at 81 Park Street in Brookline, a block from Coolidge Corner. It was less than three miles on a straight shot up Beacon Street to Little, Brown, and a block from the Green Line of Boston's subway system, the MBTA, which had a station at Park Street on the Boston Common, a stone's throw from my new office. The apartment was old but spacious—seven rooms not counting the bathroom—and came at the reasonable price of $400 per month, including old-fashioned steam heat. That was less than we had been paying in Washington. I had received a nice pay raise when I accepted the new job, so it seemed that life was about to take another good turn.

But there were problems. My new job was very demanding, and being on "the inside" meant that I was now engaged more in corporate politics than selling books, or so it seemed

to me. But none of that concerns Victoria in terms of this
story—beyond her worrying about the stress I was under—so
I won't dwell on it here. Besides, the more challenging it
was at work, the sweeter the homecoming in the evening.
Fortunately, I inherited from my father the ability to draw a
thick line in the sand between my professional and personal
lives. Although on any given day he worked under far greater
pressure than I ever have, I rarely saw him bring those pressures home with him on the commuter train to Manchester.
Admittedly, two double vodka martinis every evening helped
smooth the rough edges for him. For me, being able to be
home with Victoria most evenings, enjoying a glass or two
of wine together before supper, and then, afterward, taking a
ten-minute stroll to the Ice Cream Factory a half-mile farther
down Beacon Street (alas, no jamoca almond fudge on its
menu) was usually enough to right every wrong.

The main problem we had at that time was with our
landlords, who lived in a comparable apartment directly
above ours. (There was a third apartment above theirs.)
Max, who was approaching fifty, was short and squat and,
to put it kindly, not terribly attractive. His wife, Jenny, was
younger, petite, and far more becoming, with dark features
and long, raven hair that betokened the hot blood running
in her veins. And the heat was on too many nights as the
two of them went at it upstairs in a cacophony of screams
and objects crashing against walls. Victoria and I didn't
know whether to laugh or call the police. The next morning, invariably, the two of them would walk down the wide
stairwell smiling and sometimes holding hands, as if nothing
out of the ordinary had happened the previous night. For

them, nothing extraordinary *had* happened. It was simply their way of communicating with each other. As Victoria often said, life is full of diversity and interpretations.

Jenny liked Victoria a lot (who didn't?) and often invited her to go shopping. On one outing that included lunch at Veronique, a classy restaurant in Coolidge Corner, Jenny revealed some rather intimate details about her marriage. Victoria was used to this sort of thing; people used her as a sounding board because they knew she would listen and be discreet and pass on nothing to anyone except perhaps to me. Everyone seemed to trust her implicitly, as, of course, I did. In any event, it must have been quite a conversation, because that evening Victoria gave me a bemused look when I asked her about her lunch date.

"What?" I asked when she delayed spilling the beans.

She placed her hand on my arm. "Do you know what Max says to Jenny to get her revved up for lovemaking?"

"I can't imagine," I said, grimacing. "And I don't want to know."

"Oh, I think you do," Victoria replied impishly.

"All right, then. What does he say?" I took a good slug of wine and braced myself.

"Two words: 'Get ready.'"

I blew out my mouthful of wine and laughed uproariously along with Victoria. "Is that foreplay or a threat?" I managed at length, igniting another round of laughter. And of course the dire threat "get ready" had to be carried forward between us — and so it was, for many years.

∽

A highlight of 1980 was a trip to California that we tied to a publishing convention in Los Angeles. While I attended the four-day event, Victoria was in Arizona visiting with her sister Mary, Mary's husband, Dick, and their two children, Kelli and Brian. As soon as the convention was over, I hopped a plane from LAX to Phoenix to join them. I rented a car for ten days and then drove to the Crains' lovely home in Scottsdale, where Victoria and I stayed for two more days before packing up the car with our luggage and Mary and Dick's camping gear, on loan to us, and heading back to Los Angeles.

The evening before we left we attended one of Brian's tee-ball games. As a reference to how much time has passed since that evening, when Brian came up to bat he was not much taller than the tee! But his swing was true, and I remember him giving the ball quite a ride.

Los Angeles was not our ultimate destination, although we spent a day there. Nor was San Francisco, although we spent two days in that picturesque city where your aunt Cris had attended college to major in Spanish while chasing down the Kingston Trio. Victoria and I had a great time doing touristy things such as enjoying an Irish coffee at the legendary Buena Vista Café and a seafood dinner at the equally legendary Scoma's on Fisherman's Wharf. And as was true whenever we visited a new city, Victoria insisted we take a narrated bus tour—a strategy I highly recommend to you. Our ultimate destination, however, was Yosemite National Park. Victoria had reserved a spot in the campground for three nights back in February, and we had been planning what we would do there ever since.

A visit to Yosemite should be on everyone's bucket list, and I hope it is on yours. Trying to describe Yosemite in words simply isn't possible. Even photos can't do it justice, although Ansel Adams and other gifted photographers have taken a good stab at capturing the majestic panorama that greets the eyes and fills the senses at every turn. It's not just the staggering beauty of the Sierra Nevada, the waterfalls cascading off towering granitic rock formations, the imposing three-thousand-foot El Capitan monolith, and the forests of ancient giant sequoia trees. Once we were inside the seven-square-mile Yosemite Valley (1 percent of the park's acreage), Victoria and I found something innately spiritual, something that perhaps native Indians could grasp but was utterly beyond the verbal expression of two mortals from Boston. When we arrived at our designated campsite and began pitching our tent, we said hardly a word to each other, so mesmerized were we by the beauty and sanctity of our surroundings.

Those three days are among the most memorable of our thirty-five years together. Each morning Victoria woke up early to lay a fire, prepare a breakfast of blueberry pancakes with warm maple syrup, and get the day rolling. My job was to make coffee and pack a lunch for us, but Victoria insisted on taking charge of those chores as well and adding her always welcomed personal touch—a habit no doubt formed during her days as a Campfire Girl and as a camp counselor in Maine. After breakfast we would set off for a long hike, a picnic lunch, a swim in a secluded lake, and, always, photography—roll after roll after roll.

We both hated to see the three days end. Rarely have

Man and Nature been in such harmony, at least in our experience. But we still had a day in Palm Springs to look forward to before heading back to Boston, as well as two days in Scottsdale with family. And those aren't bad places and bad ways to decompress!

⌒⌒

That summer and fall brought us more than the usual share of misfortunes. The first and potentially most precarious was a medical diagnosis that Victoria had a tumor growing on her right ovary. When she began experiencing some discomfort in her abdomen, we made an appointment with a highly recommended physician at Massachusetts General. He referred us to a surgeon in the hospital, an elderly, kindly man who informed us, after he had conducted a series of tests, that the tumor was benign. Although he had previously told us that he was quite certain that would be the case, the relief Victoria and I felt as we sat across from him in his office was palpable.

"However," the surgeon cautioned, "although the growth is benign, I strongly recommend you have it removed. If you don't, it will almost certainly cause complications in the future. To remove it, we will have to remove the ovary. You will want a second opinion, of course."

"Of course," I said. "But if the second opinion concurs with yours, Victoria and I have already agreed we want you to perform the procedure." I glanced at Victoria and then back at him. "What is the downside, Doctor? Are there risks involved?"

The surgeon shook his head. "The procedure is quite

straightforward. There should be no risk. There is a down-side, however." He eyed us both solemnly before shifting his gaze solely to Victoria. "Do you want to have children, Mrs. Hammond?"

"Yes, we do," Victoria said quietly. "Very much."

"You still can," the surgeon assured her. "After the surgery you will still have one healthy ovary. But with only one ovary it will be harder to conceive."

Victoria didn't blink. "Then we'll just have to try twice as hard, won't we," she said, not as a question.

A slight smile formed on the surgeon's mouth. "Well, that's certainly one way of looking at it. And a rather healthy one at that."

Victoria nodded at him and then flashed me one of her brilliant smiles. "Get ready," she said.

That remark was quintessential Victoria. Whereas I was one to fret and fume in the face of adversity (not so much these days), Victoria was always grace, reason, and calm personified. No matter how bad the situation might be, she would say, "We have each other. What else do we need?" Or, "We must put our trust in God." Even during the later years when our world flipped over and came crashing down upon us, she said repeatedly, "Don't worry, Dearheart. Our love will see us through."

It always did. And it always will.

⌒

One afternoon later that fall I was working in my office on Beacon Street when I received a call from Victoria. Her voice had a raw edge that I had seldom heard before.

"What is it, Dearheart?" I asked.

"I just came home from food shopping."

"Yes. And?"

"We've been robbed. The place is a mess."

"Go outside," I said, jumping up from my chair. "I'll call the police. Wait for me on the sidewalk. I'm on my way home."

Forget the subway. I hailed a taxi and was at the apartment in ten minutes. Victoria was right. The apartment was a mess. Drawers had been ripped out and clothes were strewn all over the floor. After we surveyed the full extent of the loss and damage, I took Victoria in my arms and she started crying—for the first time in my experience.

"They found my jewelry box," she managed between sobs. "They took everything. They took my engagement ring."

I pray this sort of thing never happens to any of you, or to anyone else I hold dear. It's hard to articulate the sense of violation and outrage Victoria and I felt on that day and on the days that followed. I didn't care much about the theft of our television or other such items. They were replaceable. But the theft of Victoria's engagement ring was difficult to bear. In a real sense, it was a defilement of her very person, and of the close bond between us. I had never felt such fury boiling within me.

The police came, but they never did track down the perpetrators or recover any of the stolen items. The break-in at 81 Park Street was simply another sad statistic in Boston's burgeoning police crime log.

The burglary did help us make an important decision. Clearly it was time to move out of the city and into the suburbs. The question was, where? The North Shore, where

I was born and raised, was not a possibility. In my youth Man-chester had been a sleepy Cape Ann village of twenty-five hundred permanent residents and perhaps another two thousand summer residents. But in the free-spending '80s the town was "discovered" by parvenus who converted quaint, tasteful New England seaside homes into gaudy rock star–type mansions, changed the name of the town to a tally-ho "Manchester-by-the-Sea," and otherwise espoused the yuppie (young urban professional) lifestyle of the rich and famous—or those seeking to be accepted by this elite group of hobnobs via the cascade of easily available credit. Other North Shore communities had undergone a similar transformation, as had many of the western suburbs, and Victoria and I wanted none of them. That left the South Shore.

I was quite familiar with the South Shore, especially the town of Hingham, through a close and continuing affection for the Dana family, who for many years lived on Fearing Road. On many occasions as a teenager I had sailed my O'Day 23 back and forth between Hingham and Manches-ter. Hingham was and still is (as you well know) a lovely and relatively unpretentious seacoast town eighteen land miles southeast of Boston. The neighboring coastal towns of Cohasset, Scituate, and Duxbury are also lovely, but Victoria and I were smitten by Hingham during our Sunday drives through the area.

Property everywhere on the South Shore was undervalued compared with other Boston suburbs for one simple reason: whereas the northern and western suburbs had extensive commuter rail lines and other means of mass transit, in 1980 the South Shore had one slow-moving commuter tub that sailed each morning at 7:10 (assuming the pilot hadn't over-slept) for Rowes Wharf in Boston and left for the return trip at 5:20. The Southeast Expressway, which in theory whisked drivers from Boston down to the Cape and back, was so clogged during rush hours that locals called it the world's largest parking lot. So, demand for homes on the South Shore was limited, and that kept home prices reasonable.

But while prices in Hingham were lower than elsewhere, the real bugaboo to buying a home in 1980 and 1981 was the interest rate on home mortgages—as high as 18 percent even for those with good credit. If you didn't want to pay an exorbitant amount in interest, you had to put up a lot of the principal. And a lot of principal was something that Victoria and I didn't have.

⌒

Once again Fate played a hand, although not in the way we expected or ever would have wanted. In late November 1980 my beloved uncle Lansing suffered a massive heart attack while working in the Maine woods. My parents were there and quickly called for an ambulance, which took a while to get down to Hancock Point from Ellsworth.

My mother called me at work, and Victoria and I immedi-ately left to visit Lance in the hospital. Sadly, it would be our last visit with him. Lance seemed to be recovering—he had a heart of oak and a strong will to live—but complications set in, and during his transfer to the Eastern Maine Medical Center in Bangor, which had better facilities, Lance started hemorrhaging. By the time the ambulance arrived at the hospital, Lance had passed on, at age seventy-five.

Several months later our family lawyer informed me that Lance had left me and my two sisters a modest inheritance. It proved to be enough for Victoria and me to purchase a modest home with a low mortgage. I have no doubt that Lance fully approved of that use of his gift to us.

Chapter 6

As I said in the Preface, one of my objectives in writing this book is to explain to you boys why I believe our marriage was so successful and why it will endure forever. I hope my insights will be both interesting and beneficial to you as you contemplate your own relationships—past, present, and future.

In response you might say, "Dad, it's obvious why you and Mom had such a good marriage. You loved each other so much."

That statement is certainly true, but it is far too simple an answer. In theory, at least, everyone loves his or her spouse very much. But in my opinion—formulated over a lifetime of reading, listening, and observing—precious few people on Earth ever experience the sort of relationship that Victoria and I shared for thirty-five years and continue to share today.

In earlier chapters I alluded to several reasons why I believe Victoria and I were able to fashion a marriage for the ages. In later chapters I will allude to others. But certainly one factor that deserves special emphasis is my use of the collective "we" rather than the singular "I" that started in the first months of our marriage. This may seem like a simple admission, but for many men (and increasingly for many women) subjugating one's ego in such a way is not a natural impulse. A man's "alpha male ego" continuously asserts itself and claims priority and predominance over all comers, including those who are closest to him in blood and law: his wife and children. When it came to your mother, this sort of macho perspective was not an issue. My ego has been entirely absorbed in her since the very beginning, meaning that my greatest source of pride in life is that your mother was/is my wife and the mother of my children.

I believe I can say that Victoria felt the same about me as a husband and father. Such a mutual perspective lays a firm foundation for a strong and enduring relationship that in turn lays a firm foundation for raising children healthy in mind and spirit. I realize that many people—perhaps the vast majority of people—find this difficult if not impossible to do, especially in this secular, materialistic, "I'm up, so pull up the ladder" age in which we live. On the surface, it can seem hard to give so much of yourself to someone else while demanding or expecting nothing in return. But deep down, you receive so *much* in return when you give an integral part of yourself to another human being, especially when that human being is a person you love more than life itself.

Now, on with our story . . .

Six months before Lance passed on, I was appointed
national sales manager of the trade (as opposed to the
college, medical, or law) division of Little, Brown. While
that was a prestigious promotion in a prestigious company,
I knew from experience that the position would prove to
be ephemeral. During the previous twenty years no one
had held it for more than two years, and that included my
accomplished predecessor.

There were a number of reasons for this apparent anom-
aly, and as I said earlier, an analysis of those reasons is best
left to another author and another book. But at the heart
of the matter was the simple truth that someone had to
be held accountable if a division had a "poor" financial
year—meaning not that it lost money, but rather that it fell
short of the annual sales budget as reported at the beginning of the year to the number crunchers at Time Inc., a
budget that always showed an increase in operating profits
compared with the previous year. (Welcome to corporate
America.) In the trade division of a publishing house such
as Little, Brown, there were essentially two candidates for
the honor of falling on one's sword. Either the editor-in-
chief was blamed for signing on inferior books, or the sales
manager was blamed for being "soft" on the salespeople and
otherwise doing a poor job of supervising sales. Trouble was,
the editor-in-chief at Little, Brown was also the company's
president, chief executive officer, and publisher. *And* he was
the son of the former president who had engineered the
acquisition of Little, Brown by Time Inc. (In the 1970s and
1980s, during the first wave of publishing house acquisitions
by international conglomerates, this sort of thing was not

unusual because most well-known book-publishing houses were privately held.)

I mention this to emphasize the amount of stress that was dumped on me from the first day I took over as sales manager. My colleagues at Little, Brown with whom I worked and who worked for me were a continual source of strength and support. We did good work together; we helped place many titles on the *New York Times* bestseller list; and we shared some memorable times despite the pressure cooker forever shrieking in the kitchen. One of them, who is among the most brilliant publishing professionals I have ever known, continues to be a close friend to whom I turn for publishing and personal advice—as I did, frequently, for this book.

My primary refuge, of course, was your mother. She was always there for me, without fail. The days, hours, and minutes we shared together during those fulfilling yet challenging years became more precious with each passing day.

One great stress reliever for us was to take day trips on the weekends whenever the weather and our social calendar permitted. We were still living in Brookline then, no longer content there but not yet able to seriously contemplate moving out. By taking day trips we could leave behind our concerns in the city and focus on the joy of just being together in the close confines of the Karmann Ghia, early in the morning with a cup of Dunkin' Donuts coffee in hand, going somewhere.

Where we went was usually up to Victoria, and our options seemed limitless. One of the many joys of living in Boston is the proximity of so many world-renowned attractions. In less than a three-hour drive we could be traveling "down east" along the coast of Maine; diving deep into the woods and mountains of New Hampshire or Vermont; enjoying the rolling Berkshires in western Massachusetts; exploring the historic intrigue of a city such as Newport, Rhode Island, or Mystic, Connecticut; or beholding the seashore majesty of Cape Cod and the Islands. It takes years of planning, exploring, and day-dreaming to make a meaningful dent in the possibilities. But we had the time, and certainly we had the will. On these trips Victoria was truly in her element. She loved it all, especially if a trip included a round of antiquing and a picnic, and her joy and enthusiasm were contagious.

If we stayed overnight someplace on a Saturday—in the Green Mountains in the fall, for example, or on Martha's Vineyard in the summer—we generally stayed at an inn or a bed and breakfast rather than a motel or hotel. Victoria insisted on that. It cost less, and she loved the amenities that a typical country inn offers: quilts on the bed, fresh flowers on a table, and home-baked pastries for breakfast. For many years we talked about buying and running a country inn together. It was a fantasy, of course, but one we loved to contemplate. Over the years we came to know several New England inn owners quite well, and from what we could determine, they had no life in the summer and no money in the winter—unless the inn happened to be located near a ski slope à la *White Christmas*. Besides, for that line of work one of us needed to be handy with tools, and neither of us was. And I could not sing like Bing Crosby (as you know, I am essentially tone-deaf) and

Victoria could not dance like Rosemary Clooney, although, bless her, she came close.

As a side note, *White Christmas* was one of Victoria's favorite movies, alongside any movie starring Fred Astaire. Among her favorite singers were Bing, Andy Williams, Perry Como, and Johnny Mathis. She also enjoyed the music of Peter, Paul and Mary, Peter and Gordon, the Association, and Simon and Garfunkel, and she played their songs on the guitar both solo and in a small group with other would-be folksingers she put together in Howells. One of those in her group was Pat Leavell (née Brodecky). From what I hear, "Birdie" played a mean guitar. The group rarely went anywhere beyond someone's living room or garage, but they had a lot of fun getting together, plucking on the strings, and belting out the tunes.

More recent music—the kind you boys listened to during your teenage years—made her physically ill. "That's not music; that's noise," she would complain. And she refused to watch teenagers dancing either live in a dance hall or on television, which she rarely watched. ("TV is for idiots," she was wont to say.) To her traditionalist spirit, such grotesque gyrations were not a form of dance; they were proof of social degeneration.

Her favorite bandleader? Lawrence Welk, of course.

Another fantasy of ours at the time was to pick up stakes and move to Australia for several years. We chose Australia for several reasons, not the least of which was the fact that my uncle, Marshall Green, had recently served as the U.S. ambassador to Canberra. Victoria checked out several books from the library and studied up on the possibilities.

What she discovered was what our son Churchill rediscov-ered many years later: it was and continues to be extremely difficult for a foreigner to find work there. An Australian company (or a sheep farm or a surfing school) can com-pensate an American worker with room and board, but it cannot pay a salary. And a niece and nephew of a former U.S. ambassador to the country would receive no special privileges or consideration—which, of course, is exactly as it should be.

Victoria and I were not really disappointed. We knew we were daydreaming, and we also knew that the time for such a move had passed us by. This sort of thing is best done in a person's early to mid-twenties rather than in the early to mid-thirties. We didn't need either set of parents or anyone else to tell us that. Still, it was good to dream.

It is always good to dream.

And sometimes dreams come true.

I should know: I married the woman of my dreams.

Chapter 7

As the winter cold and snow of 1981 yielded grudgingly to spring warmth, rain, and blossoms—as New England winters generally do—Victoria and I took heart in the prospect of buying a house in the suburbs and moving out of the city. It wasn't just a question of saying good riddance to Brookline and living someplace else. There was more to it than that. Essentially, buying a house would give us a sense of permanency that we had never had. Granted, my new position at Little, Brown was the antithesis of job security, and a career move was almost certainly lurking in my not-too-distant future. But you can't sail in stormy waters forever, unsure of your compass bearing. At some point you have to seek out a sheltered cove, drop anchor, and take stock of your surroundings. Stated another way, the one constant in life—the one thing we can all depend on to happen—is change. Hanging on for dear life to "what is" often brings disappointment and frustration on a grand scale.

So we decided to drop anchor in the greater Boston area. It was where we both wanted to live for the foreseeable future and, God willing, start raising a family. In the meantime, Victoria would finally be able to pursue a job, something I knew she wanted to do but until now had not had the sense of permanency to attempt. Within three and a half years she had moved from Kansas City to McLean to Alexandria to Brookline, and was about to move to a new location. Much of her time since our wedding had been spent packing and unpacking and then packing again. Being the perfectionist she was, she wanted whatever apartment or house we occupied to be as well settled and designed as possible under the circumstances, and it was primarily on these efforts that she focused her creative energy. Certainly she was looking forward to applying that energy and skill to a house of her own. But she was also looking forward to landing a job and contributing to our financial well-being. We had set our sights on the South Shore of Boston, and while we were always prepared to consider other locations according to new information provided by a realtor or a particular house we saw, we concentrated our search in Hingham.

Our first step was to find a good realtor. Several editors at Little, Brown who lived on the South Shore steered us to a company based in Cohasset, an attractive coastal town adjacent to Hingham. It turned out to be a good business relationship. The soaring interest rates had made it a buyer's market, and there weren't many potential buyers out there. Our real estate agent was a kind, matronly woman who had lived in the area her entire life and had a wealth of information to offer us as we toured South Shore communities in her Mercedes on weekends. She knew that we preferred Hingham and approved of our choice. But she claimed she wanted to give us a good look at the entire South Shore real estate market so we could be sure. Frankly, I think she enjoyed Victoria's company and didn't want us to find a house too quickly. During those outings I sat quietly in the comfortable backseat while the two of them chattered away in the front seat discussing a wide variety of topics, many of which had nothing to do with real estate. She often treated us to lunch at a local eatery renowned for its clam chowder after Victoria confessed to her that a steaming bowl of homemade New England clam chowder was among her favorite meals.

We invested perhaps three months of Saturdays and Sundays that spring and early summer touring Cape Cod–style homes in Duxbury, ranch-style homes in Cohasset, and sea captains' homes in Hingham. We were tempted by many of these properties, but we held out. I knew Victoria was enjoying the process immensely; we were both learning a great deal about the region in which we would soon be living; the realtor seemed in no hurry to close a deal; and that seafood restaurant truly was good. Then, on a bright sunny day in late June, we found our house.

Our real estate agent later told us that she had been "saving" this one for the right moment. She had come to know us quite well by then, and she both understood and appreciated Victoria's preference for traditional settings.

"You may want to ignore the kitchen décor of this next house," she announced as we took a left off South Street in Hingham and drove up Lafayette Avenue, named after the marquis de Lafayette, who, during the Revolutionary War, had paid a visit to Hingham resident Brig. Gen. Benjamin

Lincoln, General Washington's second in command at York-town. (It was Lincoln, not Washington, who accepted Lord Cornwallis' sword of surrender.) "It's called the Sprague House," she informed us, "because it was originally built in 1920 by the Sprague family."

By Hingham standards a house built in 1920 was consid-ered new. Many of the homes within a stone's throw of the Sprague House were constructed in the 1600s. Of course, that was the appeal.

At the top of a hill Lafayette Avenue veers sharply to the right. As the Mercedes made the turn, there, a hundred feet in front of us stood an eye-catching red brick, white-trimmed, black-shuttered Georgian-style house. Out in front, ten feet from the front door, was a self-contained garden thick with tall, multicolored perennial flowers behind a For Sale sign. Victoria gave me a quick glance; in reply I gave her a slight nod. I could see she was excited.

I don't need to describe this property to you boys, because you remember it well. What you can't recall is the kitchen as we first saw it. Our agent was right. It was *bizarre*. Not only was the room painted black, there were little square mirrors all around its perimeter. Victoria and I looked at each other with the same sense of stupefaction and with the same thought in mind: maybe in the bedroom, but in the *kitchen?* There's simply no accounting for taste.

The décor on the second floor and in the basement was fine, at least in comparison with the kitchen. And as the young couple selling the house had no children, everything seemed to be in good shape. No doubt it would take some work and money to put the house the way we wanted it, but

unlike that apartment on Chestnut Street, it didn't take
much imagination to see the interior of this house in an
entirely different light and color combination.

We told the realtor we were interested and requested an
inspection. And we told her we wanted time to talk it over.
She understood, of course, and told us that she would await
our call.

In fact we had made up our minds to buy the house
before we left it that day. The first question Victoria put
to me once we were back on our own and had ordered a
drink at a local coffee shop was not, "What do you think?"
or "How do you think the inspection will go?" but rather,
"Shall we paint or wallpaper the kitchen?"

That settled that.

The asking price was $120,000. Through our realtor we
offered $90,000 and ultimately reached a compromise at
$96,500. The house was ours contingent on bank financing.
But thanks to the largesse of both our families—particularly,
in this case, Uncle Lance—that did not pose a problem.

The closing was set for at 4 p.m. on August 9, 1981, at
Brookline Savings Bank on Coolidge Corner. It went off
without a hitch, and after a celebratory drink at a local bar,
Victoria and I returned to our apartment for the last time.
The next day was moving day, and I had taken a personal day
off from work to participate in the grand event. The moving
van showed up at 11 a.m., and an hour or so later Victoria
was waving goodbye from the Ghia to Max and Jenny standing on the sidewalk. Max's face was expressionless, as it usu-

ally was in public, but as we drove away I saw Jenny swipe at a tear. That tear, I can assure you, was not for the loss of me.

By the end of the day we had our furniture, such as it was, installed if not yet properly positioned in our new home, and we had walked down the hill to get a few supplies from a small grocery store in what locals referred to as "the village," even though it was clearly a good-sized town. In 1981 Hingham had a population of twenty thousand scattered over a large geographical area. Our new home was in "historic Hingham," an area that in the 1600s included most of the original settlement. For dinner we walked to a cozy restaurant by the harbor that specialized in lightly sautéed smelts when those small fish were in season, which they were in midsummer. Tired but happy beyond words, we shared a delicious meal reinforced by a bottle of chardonnay—homeowners together in a seaside town we had already come to love after being in residence for just a few hours. During the past twenty-four hours we had made quite a change in our compass course; the sails had shifted over, and we could feel the proverbial sun and wind at our back.

⌒⊃

Reality set in the next morning as Victoria got to work putting the house to rights and I foolishly decided to test the theory of why property values in the South Shore communities were depressed compared with those in other Boston suburbs. We now had two cars—Cris' in-laws in Manchester owned an old Buick that they rarely used, and we had bought it from them at a more than reasonable price—so off I went down Main Street through South Hingham to Norwell, a route through what *Town and Country* magazine has labeled "the quintessential New England town at Christmas," and from there onto Route 3. I left home at 7:15, thinking that would give me ample time to drive the eighteen miles to Boston, park the car in the Underground Garage on the Common, and be at my desk before 8:30. I make it a point never to be late for work or for an appointment, but I was late for work that morning. I walked into 34 Beacon Street at 9:10. The next day, and most days thereafter, I left home at 7 a.m. and drove a back road to Braintree to ride the Red Line of the MBTA to Park Street.

On Fridays I generally took the commuter boat to and from Long Wharf. I would have done that every day, but the old tub left the dock in Boston precisely at 5:20. To catch it, I had to leave Little, Brown promptly at 5 p.m. and hoof it to the waterfront. As appealing as that hour-long commute among the picturesque Boston Harbor Islands might be—especially in the summer sitting up on deck with a beer or glass of wine in hand—it was not good form for the sales manager of a company to be seen hightailing it from his office at quitting time!

After I left the house that first day, Victoria placed a call to Paul Morgan, a painter and jack-of-all-trades who lived in the neighboring coastal town of Hull. He had come highly recommended to us by our real estate agent, with the caveat that Paul's friendly disposition and high-quality work put him in high demand throughout the South Shore. Likely we would not be able to make an appointment with him for weeks or even months. Undaunted, Victoria called him at his home and left a message for him.

Over a glass of wine together that evening Victoria told me that she had called Paul Morgan.

"Did he return the call?" I asked.

"Yes, he did. This afternoon."

"That was nice of him. What did he say?"

"He's coming by at nine o'clock on Saturday morning," she answered nonchalantly. "He sounds perfect for us. I'm looking forward to meeting him."

"So is everyone else on the South Shore," I quipped. "So you spun your magic web again, did you?"

In response, she flashed me one of her brilliant smiles.

Paul showed up right on schedule on Saturday, and I knew I was going to like him the moment I saw him get out of his station wagon and walk toward the house. He was perhaps fifty years old, tall and lean, with the leathery palms of a master craftsman and the kind and caring eyes of a priest. Most people when you meet them try to project an image that may or (in most cases) may not be an accurate depiction of their true character. Not so with Paul Morgan. There was not an ounce of pretension in his mind, body, or spirit. What you saw was what you got, and what you got, you liked. You sensed it immediately, and it put you entirely at your ease.

Your mother had the same quality.

Paul came in through the front entrance, which we rarely used because it faced a grassy slope where the entrance to (or exit from) Lafayette Avenue used to be before it was moved. The kitchen entrance leading to and from our free-standing garage was much more convenient.

When Paul walked into the kitchen, his eyes went wide and his jaw dropped. Then he burst out laughing. "What is *this?*" he asked.

"This is the kitchen, Paul," Victoria said matter-of-factly. "Your first assignment."

Paul gave Victoria a gentle look, because he was a gentle man. "Yes, ma'am," he said humbly but with a grin. "I promise to try my hardest."

We gave Paul a thorough tour of the house and then invited him back into the kitchen for a cup of coffee. To our surprise, he accepted. We realized that he was much in demand, and he had already granted us almost an hour of his time. So we were flattered.

It turned out Paul liked Cremora in his coffee, and we didn't have Cremora—or much else, for that matter. After all, we had just moved in. But Victoria being Victoria, she apologized profusely.

"That's okay, Mrs. Hammond," Paul said. "Milk will do fine for today. Just don't make that mistake again," he added with a chuckle.

We must have talked for another hour. Most of the conversation was about our family, his wife and family, and the good life on the South Shore. If Paul had the world waiting for him on his doorstep, he gave no indication of it. It was as though waiting for us to arrive on the South Shore was his *raison d'être*. We did discuss business now and then—Paul wanted to know if we would be working with an interior decorator, for example, although he quickly appreciated Victoria's own artistry and grasp of colors—but never, not once that day, did we discuss the cost of his services. I didn't care how much he charged, and because I understood the small husband-wife signals so well by this time, I knew that Victoria too would beg, borrow, or steal to have this man work on our house. There was one question we had to ask, however, and we finally got around to asking it.

"Paul," Victoria said, "Bill and I want you to work with us on this house."

"Are you sure?" he asked. "You might want to discuss it between yourselves in private. And of course I am willing to supply as many references as you'd like."

"From what we hear," I said, "*we're* the ones who should be supplying the references."

Paul got a good laugh out of that remark.

"Seriously, Paul," I added, "we're sure, no matter what the wait may be."

"What is the wait going to be?" Victoria inquired cautiously. We both feared the worst—that we'd have visions of sugar plum fairies dancing in our heads before we would see Paul again. And if so, we'd be stuck with this bizarre kitchen décor through the holidays and well into the New Year.

"Well," Paul said softly, his gaze drifting up to the ceiling as he did some mental figuring, "it *is* tight at the moment, I can't deny that. But I can move things around a little. Change an appointment or two here and there." His eyes twinkled as his gaze settled back on me and then on Victoria. "What are they going to do? Fire me? So let's see. Today is Saturday. I'll need a little time . . . What say we begin a week from Monday?"

Victoria gave Paul one of her best smiles ever. "That will do fine," she said.

⌒

The next day, Sunday, we received a call from a man who many years earlier had launched his career working for my father in the Boston office of White, Weld & Company. He now managed his own investment company in Boston and had heard of our recent move to Hingham. He and his wife, Joan, lived only about a mile from us. He extended an invitation to come over for dinner the next Saturday and we gratefully accepted.

It was a lovely summer evening. We had cocktails by the pool—Mike made a James Bond–inspired martini—and then dinner inside in their richly appointed dining room. When Victoria commented on how exquisite everything looked, it came out that Joan, a truly lovely woman, was an interior decorator of some renown.

"Please understand," Mike was quick to point out. "We did not invite you here tonight to solicit new business. We invited you here to solicit new friends. I will always be indebted to your father, Bill, for what he taught me about business, and Joanie and I have been looking forward to meeting you and Victoria. We are delighted you decided to live in Hingham."

"Understood, Mike," I said.

"However," Joan put in, "if I can be of any help to you, I would be happy to do so on a strictly gratis basis. In fact, I have taken the liberty of writing down a few names of local painters and whatnot should you have need of one. I highly recommend them all."

"That was kind of you, Joan," Victoria said. "But we already have a painter. He's starting on Monday."

"Oh? That was quick. Who did you get?"

"Paul Morgan."

Joan's jaw dropped and she nearly tipped over her wine glass. "Did you say Paul Morgan? *The* Paul Morgan?"

"Is there more than one?"

"No, but . . . but . . . didn't you just move here?"

"Ten days ago."

"Had you known Paul before?"

"No."

Joan gave Victoria a look of utter bewilderment. "You do understand, don't you, that Paul is one of the most popular men on the South Shore. He's on the top of everyone's list, including the one I made for you. But I was thinking of some time next year. Even I have to wait weeks, sometimes months, to see Paul." She shook her head, still not believing. "How *on earth* did you manage it?"

"I don't know," Victoria said as I smiled inwardly. I knew *exactly* how Victoria had managed it. By just being Victoria.

"Would you like to come over to our house on Monday morning?" Victoria asked Joan. "Paul will be there at nine o'clock."

"Thank you, my dear." Joan replied without hesitation. "I wouldn't miss it for the world."

We made good friends that Saturday evening in Hingham. And Victoria's reputation in the town and throughout the South Shore had taken a giant leap forward. In the

weeks and months to come, word traveled through the
grapevine of Victoria's legendary "in" with Paul Morgan,
and some people tried to get to him through her. But that
was one game Victoria refused to play. She was very protec-
tive of our relationship with Paul.

⌒

So began a long and meaningful relationship with Joan and
Paul, especially Paul. Joan contributed a lot to the remodel-
ing of our home's interior, and not only because of her own
good taste in furniture and wallpaper. As an interior decorator she had access to designers' showrooms that offered
quality furniture to her clients at steep discounts. Normally
that discount represents the decorator's fee, but Joan
charged us next to nothing.

Paul, meanwhile, showed up for work on almost a daily
basis for three months. Early on we gave him a key to the
house, and each morning we had a pot of hot coffee on
the kitchen counter next to a mug and Cremora container,
both of which had "PAUL" written on the side in Victoria's
decorative handwriting. Even on the days he didn't come
to work on our house Paul would often stop by for a cup of
coffee. He bought all his paint at the Sherwin-Williams store
located at the bottom of our hill behind the grocery store—
and perhaps fifty feet from Talbots' first store. (Talbots is a
Hingham-based company.) It was always good to see him and
listen to his commonsense "take" on the affairs of the world.
He was thoroughly aware of local, state, national, and global
goings-on, far more than Victoria or I, and he had distinct
opinions to share with us. We learned a lot from him, and not

just about colors and the proper way to hang wallpaper. We learned a lot about life and the value of friendships too.

After two months without receiving a bill from Paul, we began to worry. Victoria and I had a hard-and-fast rule to pay service people first. A utility company, for example, can absorb a slight delay in payment, but a self-employed service provider generally cannot. We had built a "war chest" from which to pay Paul and other workers, but the longer we went without paying, the more nervous we became. So one Saturday morning over a cup of coffee with Paul, we finally broached the subject.

"Funny you should ask," he said. "I was just working on your bill last evening." He reached into his shirt pocket. "Here it is, to date."

Tentatively Victoria and I peered at the plain piece of white paper with a few calculations noted in pencil and a "grand total" amount underlined at the bottom. We were shocked.

"Paul," I said moments later, "I've rarely said this to anyone, but you're not charging us enough. This can't be much beyond your own costs."

Paul gave me a knowing smile. "Compensation comes in many forms, Bill," he said. "Money is just one of them. I charge enough to get by. What more do I need?"

As I struggled to answer that question, he added with a broad grin. "Besides, I charge the fat cats around here a slightly higher fee."

"I won't tell Joanie," Victoria said, flashing him one of her smiles.

"Please don't." Paul said, and we shared a good laugh.

As the years went by we saw less of Paul, although Victoria kept his mug and Cremora handy on the off chance that he might drop by. Not long before we moved from Hingham to Minneapolis, Paul came by the house to tell us that he was retiring and moving with his wife to Florida.

"I still have the key to your house," he told us, "and of course you can have it back. But if you don't mind, I'd like to keep it as a memento of our time together."

Victoria simply nodded. Emotion had clogged her throat.

Several years later we received word that Paul had passed on from cancer. That evening I went into the kitchen as Victoria was preparing dinner for you boys. Her back was to me, but I could hear her weeping softly. When I came up to her and gently placed my hands on her shoulders, she turned around and melted into my arms, sobbing.

"I'm sorry to cry," she managed at length.

"Don't be," I said, as much to comfort myself as my wife. "Paul was my friend too."

Throughout the thirty-five years Victoria and I were together, we met many people of many impressive stripes and backgrounds. In our eyes, Paul Morgan will forever stand head and shoulders above the crowd. I wish you could have known him.

Chapter 8

Early in 1981 I made the decision to attend graduate school in business administration. I realized what signal that decision would send to the Little, Brown brass—publishing sales managers do not, as a rule, go to business school—but I figured that having an MBA, worthwhile in and of itself, would expand my job prospects when I left the company.

Since I would be attending school at night, I had basically two options: Boston University and Babson College. B.U. has an excellent program, and it made sense in that I was already working downtown. But who knew how much longer that would last? Besides, I was drawn inexorably to Babson's lovely and intimate campus nestled in the rolling hills of Wellesley in Boston's western suburbs. And its internationally recognized specialty is in entrepreneurship, a subject of considerable interest to me. (Although book publishing is one of the oldest industries in the world, every book published is essentially a new and untested product.) So Babson it was if I could get in. And I did.

Because more than ten years had elapsed since I graduated from college, I had to take noncredit tutorials in
mathematics, economics, and computer science before I
could start on the twenty core courses necessary to graduate, ten of which were mandatory and ten of which were
electives. I started in the fall of 1981 by taking the three
tutorial courses. On the two evenings a week I attended
classes I had to leave home at 6:30 in the morning to get
a jump on rush hour traffic and did not return home until
9:30 that night.

Victoria, meanwhile, was busy working on the house with
Paul and Joan, and each day we could see progress. A wonderful transformation was taking place right before our eyes
in a space that was wholly ours. Upstairs, on the second
floor, were four corner rooms: our bedroom, Victoria's dress-
ing room, a guest room, and a room I wanted to convert
into an artist's studio. As a student at the Kansas City Art
Institute, Victoria had specialized in painting and also in
printmaking, a process of creating artworks by reproducing
images on paper. She had a great talent for it, as you boys
know. One need only look around our home to see that talent framed on the walls. Victoria vetoed the studio idea. A
considerable investment would be required to procure the
necessary equipment, but that was not what deterred her.
It was having the time required to do it right; and when it
came to her art, Victoria was a perfectionist's perfectionist.

"Printmaking is not a profession," she often told me. "It's
an obsession. That's fine when you're in college and you
have the time and freedom to devote to it. I feel blessed
to have had that time. But my emphasis now must be on

you and our future and the family we want to have. I can teach art to our children. That will be reward enough for all those hours of training and education." Try as I might to change her mind, she remained adamant. And I confess to being utterly undone by her unselfish rationale. Who on this earth forsakes a God-given talent finely honed at the highest level of academia in order to devote her life to those she loves?

Your mother, for one.

⌒

During this time, Victoria joined the Junior League of Boston, an organization of women committed to volunteer-ism and to developing the potential of women. Joining the Junior League allowed her to become more deeply involved in the greater Boston community and to develop a number of important contacts. In my experience, women who join their local chapter of the Junior League are women of supe-rior intellect and rectitude. Victoria thrived in that environ-ment, and through it she made many friends in Hingham and elsewhere, several of whom were soon to become very influential in her life.

During the winter and spring of 1982 Victoria was having so much fun doing what she was doing that she started feeling guilty again about not having a job. No matter how much I tried to convince her that her work on our home was adding considerably to our net worth, she was never entirely consoled by my words. Besides, she knew what I had done on January 1 of that year: I had typed out my resignation letter from Little, Brown. I planned to deliver it to my boss on August 12. That date would allow me to give two weeks' notice and collect my three weeks' vacation pay for the year before starting a full-time regimen at Babson in late September. Taking one or two courses per semester would take too long to graduate, so I had decided to become preemptive and take the proverbial plunge.

"I need to have a job by then, certainly," Victoria said to me one evening.

"You will, Dearheart," I assured her. "Even if you don't, we'll have enough cash and Time Inc. stock on hand to see us through for a few more months, at least."

I well remember that evening. I had been on a trip out to Minneapolis to sell the fall list to B. Dalton with Tony, the local Little, Brown rep, who was nearly twice my age. We had wrapped up our business earlier than expected and I had booked an earlier flight home, despite Tony's attempts to persuade me to remain in Minneapolis for another evening to share some fun time. We had already spent two days together, and I truly enjoyed Tony's company. He was a jolly man who personified Eastern European courtesy when such courtesy was required. But I knew from hard experience that his interpretation of "travel and entertainment" was taking a cab into the seedier areas of the city to watch blue movies, the bluer the better. I preferred being home with my wife.

This was not an isolated incident. During the course of my professional life I have had many occasions to travel overnight on business. Most of my colleagues view such travel as a legitimate excuse to escape the responsibilities and daily grind of home life. You get to go to preferred cities (usually), stay at a nice hotel, and eat out at noted restaurants, all at company expense. What's not to like?

Well, nothing. But to the surprise and even consternation of my co-workers who genuinely enjoyed the corporate perk, I took an earlier-than-scheduled flight home whenever I could do so without compromising business. Victoria never encouraged me to do it. She would not have done that under any circumstances. The decision was always mine alone. Even on my last business trip as a publishing consultant—in February 2011 on behalf of Hazelden Publishing to assist in a proposed acquisition of its Florida-based distributor—I opted to return home on Friday when our business mission was fulfilled rather than spend a "free" winter Saturday on the beach at Boca Raton.

When people asked me why I always hurried home, the answer was simple. I have already alluded to it several times in this book. What it came down to is what I told a dear friend not long after Victoria and I were married. My friend had asked me to describe my wife to her. Not her physical appearance, because she had seen photographs of Victoria. She wanted me to describe Victoria's essence to her.

I thought only for a moment. "She is the giver of peace," I told her. And after all these years I can think of no better phrase to describe your mother. She *was* the giver of peace—to me, to you boys, and to countless others who knew her.

For me, she still is.

⌒つ

Here, if I may, a brief word on the delicate topic of fidelity. As you no doubt have discovered for yourselves, this world presents ample opportunities to cheat on one's spouse, especially for those, like you three, whose physical appearance has been blessed by a combination of Mother Nature and your mother's genes. I don't know if infidelity has increased in recent years, but I strongly suspect that it has. Public figures openly engage in it, and their behavior is all but glorified by the popular media. During my career I have seen more than my share of "office flings" and "nooners" that did not involve a spouse. My purpose here is not to examine the reasons why people cheat. Nor is it to condemn or pass judgment on anyone who does, or to appear in any way "holier than thou." This sort of human activity has been going on since the dawn of Man, and will continue until the twilight of Man. Each person has his or her reason for doing it. And of course I realize that not all marriages turn out well, and cheating on one's spouse can be a result of that unfortunate state of affairs as well as a cause.

You may someday be tempted, and who knows how you will respond. But for me—and I can only speak for myself— there is something infinitely sad about superficial flings. Unconditional love for another human being that is based on mutual respect, trust, sacrifice, honesty, gratitude, and loyalty is so much more nourishing to mind, body, and spirit than a brief affair. If that sounds corny, so be it. It happens to be true. How someone can cheat on someone he or she allegedly loves is beyond my ability to comprehend. I never felt even a shred of envy when I saw a colleague cheat on

a spouse in the office or while on a business trip. I felt sorry
for them. I had it far better than they did—on that day and
on every day.

Victoria felt the same way. A traditionalist in every sense
of the word, she devoutly believed, as I did and still do, that
marriage is a sacred union of two bodies and souls during
this lifetime and through all eternity.

⌒

As 1982 progressed, I felt the walls at Little, Brown closing
in on me. In early April I notified Babson that I would be
switching from part-time to full-time status as of the fall
semester. And with my decision to leave the company in
August already made, at least some of the pressure on me
had been released. I felt, in effect, like a pitcher who main-
tains a lead but who has been on the mound for a little too
long. Three years is long enough to serve in a position that
offers no opportunity for advancement in the foreseeable
future. Further, I had serious doubts that I would want a
promotion even if it were to be offered. During the previous decade two general managers of the trade division had
suffered physical calamity at much too early an age.

Victoria, meanwhile, went out job hunting. Immediately
after she graduated from the Kansas City Art Institute, she
had taught art at Penn Valley, a community college in Kansas City. While she loved practicing art, teaching it proved
to be another matter, in part because too few students
shared her passion for the subject and her commitment to
perfection. Nevertheless, she applied as an art instructor to
several schools on the South Shore but found no full-time

position available. The one opening was as a substitute teacher at Derby Academy, your future school. Victoria also applied, twice, to the Boston office of the Landmarks Commission, but at neither time was there an opening. So she broadened her search into other areas of possible employment, hoping to find something either on the South Shore or in the western suburbs of Boston.

⌒

You have heard the expression "When it rains, it pours." Its flip side is "When the clouds part, the sun shines everywhere." So it was for Victoria and me in August 1982.

A week before I planned to hand in my resignation, my secretary notified me that my boss wanted to see me in his office. The gist of the conversation was that, from the company's perspective, the time had come for me to move on. Happily, that was also my perspective.

"If you make this easy for us, Bill," the general manager said, "we will make it easy for you."

My reply, "You have no idea how easy I'm going to make this for you, John," pleased him, and so it was that I was able to work for three additional weeks and leave the company on the day I had originally indicated on my letter of resignation. And I left with a "sweetener" that was by no means a golden parachute, but which nevertheless contained a few flecks of silver. I did have mixed feelings about leaving the company on that final day. I was relieved beyond measure to be free of the pressure cooker, and I was looking forward to the future; but I truly loved the books Little, Brown published and the people I worked with.

Sadly, in several years John, the fortyish general manager, would die of throat cancer, the third general manager to be undone in that position.

When I returned home that evening to tell Victoria the news, she had big news for me. A friend named Missy whom she had met in the Junior League worked as an assistant manager at Brooks Brothers, and she had urged Victoria to apply for a position there. Her interview had been that very day.

"I got the job," she gushed when I was hardly through the kitchen door.

"What exactly is the job?" I asked.

"Well," she said, "I'm going to start as a cashier, to learn the business. But according to Missy, after a month or two, if all goes well, I will be transferred to sales in the Ladies' Department."

This was important. At the time, Brooks Brothers was a privately held company that paid handsome commissions to its salespeople in addition to a higher-than-average hourly wage. A sales position at Brooks Brothers was a highly coveted job, and salespeople rarely left the company on their own accord.

I picked her up by the hips and twirled her around in a full circle. "That's wonderful," I told her. "Congratulations. When do you start?"

"The Tuesday after Labor Day."

I made a quick mental calculation and then told her my news. "Tell you what. Give Missy a call tomorrow and see if you can start two weeks later. Don't jeopardize the job; just see what she says."

"Okay," Victoria said.

The following evening Victoria told me it was all set. That timetable actually worked better for Brooks Brothers. They had been worried they would lose Victoria if they deferred the position for too long, but the delay suited them to a tee.

The following morning I received a call in my office from the former director of the New York Graphic Society (whose books Little, Brown distributed). Tim had heard that I was soon to leave Little, Brown and he wanted me to come in for lunch with him and Harry, another former Little, Brown employee and a close friend. Naturally, I accepted.

Over lunch that Friday at the Hampshire House (the setting for the popular television sit-com *Cheers*), Tim detailed his unique and, on the surface, very interesting business plan that had the publisher acting in the role of a movie producer bringing capital, editing, and marketing together from different sources on behalf of world-class British and American authors. He and Harry had already raised a considerable sum of money and were looking to raise substantially more through a series of what are referred to in investment circles as "dog and pony shows," most of which would be held in the same room in which we were now sitting. While negotiating with the targeted authors and their agents, Tim's company would reissue the first novels of these authors in high-quality, creatively designed hardback editions.

"We need someone with hands-on sales experience," Tim told me. "Someone to sell the initial list of books to the major accounts and, more important, to give comfort to potential investors that a sales professional is on board."

When I told Tim I would soon be immersed in business school, he assured me that he and Harry understood that. Their demands on my time would be strictly limited, and he was prepared to pay me a more than generous monthly stipend to compensate me for my time. In sum, he made me an offer I couldn't refuse. My only request was that I start on October 1 rather than September 1.

"Agreed," Tim said, and the three of us shook hands.

So there Victoria and I were on a Friday evening in mid-August, as happy as two clams in the sand at high tide, as you boys used to say. In two weeks we would have three carefree weeks together, with cash in the bank and the promise of more cash to come. And the best part? At the end of the three weeks we would both be starting something new and exciting—and close to each other. As Fate would have it, Victoria's job at Brooks Brothers was in the Chestnut Hill Mall, an upscale shopping emporium a mere twenty minutes down Route 9 from Babson College. Most days we would be able to commute together.

Yes, indeed. On that Friday in August the sun was shining everywhere.

Chapter 9

In later years, as Victoria and I sat by the fire in our home in Minneapolis, we often talked about the best days of our life together. Without question our wedding day and subsequent wedding trip to St. John rank near the top. What can possibly top one euphoric moment after another, day after joyful day, in a wildly romantic setting? Just three things, of course, and those are the birthdays of you boys. Each of those three events is a God-given gift to us both for which we give eternal thanks. But right behind those unforgettable days are the three weeks Victoria and I shared starting that Friday in August 1982.

Victoria loved to travel, and travel we did. To Maine to visit my parents, and from there into Canada. To the Cape and the Islands, in particular Block Island, where we stayed in the elegant confines of the 1661 Inn. And then on to Montauk on the tip of Long Island, where we went fishing and enjoyed a picnic overlooking the rugged beauty of Gardiners Bay. When we were home in Hingham we barbequed, sailed, fished, hiked, slept late, and hosted two garden parties for our neighbors and newfound friends on the South Shore. We splurged only once, and that was to celebrate our fifth wedding anniversary—an important milestone for any couple. Victoria loved anniversaries of any kind. But none was more important to her than our wedding anniversary. We had celebrated our first and third anniversaries in New York, the latter in the Time-Life suite compliments of Saint Nick. On our second anniversary we spent a memorable weekend at the historic Jared Coffin House on Nantucket. And for our fourth we had booked two nights at the majestic Chateau Frontenac in Québec City, but never made it. When our Ghia broke down with a plugged fuel line on the Canadian border, we were forced to spend the night in a Newport, Vermont, motel and then turn around the next day after the car was finally fixed late in the afternoon. To make up for that miscue we resolved to book our fifth anniversary weekend at some extra-special place. The place we picked was The Breakers in Palm Beach, a landmark hotel opened in 1896 by Henry Flagler, real estate and railroad magnate and the founder of Standard Oil.

Mind you, had matters not turned out so fortuitously for us during the previous month we would never have considered doing something so extravagant—or doing much of anything out of the ordinary during those three weeks. Even with off-season rates and a weekend special in a room with no water view, The Breakers was one of the most expensive hotels we ever stayed in. But, oh, what a hotel! Situated at the edge of the Atlantic Ocean on 105 acres, it features spectacular views, vast expanses of green lawns and groves of stately royal palms, and impeccable service. Sometimes indulging in over-the-top opulence can rejuvenate the soul, especially when commemorating such a meaningful anniversary. Certainly it was a weekend we would hark back to for years to come.

Our plan was to fly to Palm Beach on a flight leaving Boston at noon on Friday and to return late in the day on Sunday. This weekend was two weeks before our actual anniversary on September 24, to give us a full week back in Hingham before Victoria started work at Brooks Brothers and I began business school.

But there was a problem. Weather maps showed two massive fronts approaching the mainland United States, one from the Gulf of Mexico and the other from the Caribbean, and they were predicted to converge over southern Florida late in the day on Friday and continue dumping torrents of rain on the Sunshine State throughout the weekend and into the following week.

"Should we cancel?" I asked Victoria on Wednesday. "We won't have to pay anything if we do it by six o'clock tonight."

Victoria shook her head. "No," she said adamantly. "We used our frequent flyer miles to purchase the airline tickets, and everything is all set. Besides, I can think of worse places to spend our fifth anniversary than cooped up in The Breakers."

Good point, my love. On Friday morning we drove to Logan Airport and boarded our flight for Palm Beach International.

The rain had started by the time our plane landed two and a half hours later. We got our luggage and rental car and drove through the gathering storm to The Breakers, where we received a royal welcome and keys to Room 328, a lovely nook facing west and overlooking the idyllic lawns, magnificent flora, and towering palm trees lining the sweeping front entrance of the majestic Italian Renaissance structure.

After settling in, we went down to the pool area, ordered two piña coladas from the pool bar, and sat under a cabaña talking and gazing out at the swirling whitecaps of the broiling and brooding ocean. Not Florida at its best, but also not a bad way to spend an afternoon. One cocktail led to another and the bartender asking us if he could make a dinner reservation for us anywhere in the area. We had already made a reservation in the hotel restaurant for the following evening at eight, but neither of us had much desire to drive in the raging storm to seek out another eatery. So we made a reservation at the hotel restaurant for seven o'clock that evening.

It turned out to be a good choice. The grouper and swordfish were outstanding, and Victoria pronounced the key lime pie to be among the best she had ever tasted, which was saying something. Key lime pie was one of her three signature homemade desserts—the two others being trifle pudding and hot apple crisp capped with vanilla ice cream. Any of them would have put a smile on the face of Fanny Farmer, Julia Child, or any other culinary authority. But the best part was that on Friday and Saturday nights The Breakers featured ballroom dancing with a talented Lawrence Welk-type band. After dinner we danced the night away and then walked up to our room, exhausted but elated. Outside, the wind howled and rain splattered heavily on the windowpanes.

It was a good night to snuggle.

When I awoke the next morning, I immediately sensed that something was different. It was the same sort of sense that a sailor gets when awakening at sea after the wind has shifted and the boat is on a different tack. Listening intently, I tried to figure out what, exactly, was going on—or not. Then it came to me: it was stone quiet. There was no sound whatsoever. A quick glance at the window revealed a thin line of bright light on each side of the thick shade.

I slipped out of bed and tiptoed over to the window. Drawing aside the shade, I peered out into the dawn—and was stunned by what I saw.

"What is it, Dearheart?" I heard Victoria ask me groggily. "Why up so early?"

I continued to stare outside. "Because what I'm looking at is beyond belief. There's not a cloud in the sky."

"Yeah, right," Victoria muttered.

"I'm serious. Observe." I raised the shade and instantly our room was awash in a dazzling brightness.

"My Lord, you're *right*," Victoria exclaimed, getting out of bed to join me by the window. "What a lovely, lovely day! What happened, do you think?"

I shrugged. "I'm not sure. Maybe the two storms collided and blew themselves out."

"I guess that makes sense. What should we do to celebrate?"

"I know," I said. "Let's call room service and have breakfast right here."

"Good idea," Victoria agreed. "I'll get on it."

"I'll have whatever you have. In the meantime I'll go and shave."

As I was shaving before the bathroom mirror, I heard Victoria on the phone through the open door.

"Hello? Room Service? This is Victoria Hammond in Room 328 . . . Good morning . . . I'd like to order a pot of coffee for two, two large glasses of freshly squeezed orange juice, and a key lime pie . . . No, not two slices of pie, a whole pie . . . Yes, that's right . . . No, that will be all, thank you. Good-bye."

I peered around the door opening. "Good order," I said.

Fifteen minutes later there was a gentle knock on the door and an elegantly attired waiter entered our room pushing a cart bearing a silver coffee pot, two large cut-crystal glasses of orange juice, and a silver tureen-like serving platter. Because the cart served double duty as a table, the waiter set about arranging everything in precise order, as though he were attending to the duke and duchess of Cambridge. As Victoria and I sat down across from each other, he leaned over and, with a grand flourish, whipped the silver lid off the platter.

"Your pie, madam," he announced with utmost gravity and a slight bow.

We probably could have flown to Nassau for breakfast for the price of that pie and service fee and generous tip, but I wouldn't have traded it for anything. I will forever maintain that the best breakfast ever was Victoria's seafood omelet prepared during our cook-off in Kansas City. This one was second best. Not a crumb of that pie was left, and I still smile with a surge of fond memory whenever I think about dining with my beloved in sun-washed Room 328 in The Breakers Hotel in Palm Beach, Florida.

⌒

We spent the day exploring Worth Avenue, Palm Beach's answer to Rodeo Drive in Beverly Hills and Fifth Avenue in New York as an enclave of retail establishments catering to the super rich. We didn't buy anything beyond a Christmas tree ornament (a tradition of ours when traveling), but it was fun strolling around and looking at stuff we would never be able to afford. Then again, the male dandies who were there to do some serious shopping were not strolling hand in hand with a woman like your mother. Which would you rather have: wads of cash or a woman like your mother? I know *my* answer.

That evening we kept our eight o'clock dinner reservation at The Breakers. We toyed with the notion of booking somewhere else for our official anniversary dinner because we had dined there the previous evening, but we decided to stay with what we had—which was the best. The only difference this Saturday evening was that we had champagne rather than chardonnay, and Victoria ordered the grouper and I had the swordfish. But that came out the same as the previous evening because we always shared fifty-fifty whatever we ordered.

After again dining in style, we took to the dance floor and stayed there until the band stopped playing at one o'clock. On the elevator up to the third floor, I kissed Victoria. "Tired?" I asked.

"I'm too happy to know if I'm tired," she replied.

"Then how about a walk on the beach?"

"Sounds heavenly," she said.

Quickly we changed into more casual clothes and retraced our steps to the first floor, where we walked out a side door to the pool area and down a set of stone stairs to the beach.

The beach was deserted as we walked hand in hand along the water's edge by the light of a harvest moon casting a treasure trove of sparkling diamonds on the dead-calm ocean. We could see a few lights flickering within the palm-fringed foliage, but on that gorgeous night we had the beach at Palm Beach entirely to ourselves.

"How about a swim?" Victoria suddenly suggested.

"Lead the way," I said.

Lead she did. After a quick glance up and down the beach she peeled down to bare essentials and stepped into the blood-warm water. I followed suit, and soon we were splashing about in chest-deep water. At one point I was staring out to sea at a ship's lights on the distant horizon when Victoria snuck up behind me with the intent to startle me. For the sake of propriety, I will not mention how. But as I had grown up next to the ocean on Cape Ann and learned to swim at the same time I learned to walk, I do not startle easily in water.

"Listen," I said, slowly turning around. "It might interest you to know that sharks like to feed at night, especially on young blond-haired women from Nebraska."

Lickety-split, in surges of white water, Victoria shot out of the ocean onto dry land. She turned to face me, arms akimbo. "That was a horrid thing to say," she said, but I was laughing too hard to heed her—that is, until I felt something brush against the back of my legs. It may have been my imagination, but I was not about to hang around to find out. With as much aplomb and dignity as I could muster, I waded out of the sea to join my bride on the beach.

‿◌

The next morning we packed up the rental car and, after buying some fruit and two sandwiches, drove north along the sixteen-mile barrier island that separates Palm Beach and environs from the mainland. On the island's northern tip an inlet leads in from the ocean to the Atlantic Intra-coastal Waterway, a stretch of protected water extending from Key West, Florida, to Norfolk, Virginia. It was at a dock here, many years previously, that my father and two sisters and I had met Dad's long-time friend Frank Sauer, who operated a sport-fishing boat out of Riviera Beach. As Victoria knew by this time as well, Diana and Cris had learned at an early age that when it came to Pappy and fishing, you enjoyed it whether you liked it or not. At least Captain Sauer had the good sense to hire handsome young mates, which kept Cris happy and eager for the next close encounter in the Gulf Stream.

In the ensuing years the area had been built up some—as rustic places of innate beauty usually are—but it still held great appeal. As we sat in silence on a grassy knoll under a palm tree staring down into gin-clear water in which fish small and large were swimming lazily about in search of food, Victoria sighed contentedly.

"It's beautiful," she whispered.

"Yes, Mrs. Hammond, you are," I said.

Victoria smiled at me and then rested her head gently upon my shoulder. "Tell me something?" she murmured.

"Of course. Ask away."

Her voice was barely audible. "Will the next fifty years be as wonderful as these past five years?"

I put my arm around her to draw her in closer. "How could they not be," I answered softly, "with you as my wife?"

And we sat there by the cerulean blue ocean beneath a warm Florida sun and swaying palm fronds, each of us in blissful contemplation of a long future together that we both knew would be well lived and well loved.

Chapter 10

A week after our return from Florida we began our new regimen. The thought of being back in a classroom at the ripe old age of thirty-four may be anathema to many people, but I found it highly stimulating—the horror of Statistics notwithstanding. And I was pleased to discover that there were a number of other people my age or older who were doing the same thing I was doing. In night classes there were many students in their fifties who were planning to take early retirement from companies such as Johnson & Johnson in order to launch their own entrepreneurial ventures.

Victoria flourished in her new environment as well. With the exception of several seasoned veterans in Men's Suits, the sales staff at Brooks Brothers comprised young and attractive men and women in their late twenties and early thirties who loved their job. Victoria fit right in. Shortly after her first day at work, the entire staff, including senior management, was pushing hard for her promotion to sales. It was not just her winning ways and obvious enthusiasm that won her high marks. Everyone, especially customers, immediately sensed her grasp of proper color coordination, an essential skill especially in the Ladies' Department, where a discerning clientele of all ages sought competent advice on formal wear. In that capacity Victoria was a rock star. She was a terrific salesperson because she knew her stuff and because she *cared* about both her customers and her company. Less than three weeks after her first hour as a Brooks Brothers cashier she was promoted to the coveted position of sales representative. Missy later told her that no one in the company's history had been so quickly honored. That came as a surprise to Victoria. But not to me.

Thus began a routine of commuting from Hingham north on Routes 3 and 128 during the week and often on the weekends. Victoria worked five days a week, at various hours depending on the week's schedule, and whenever possible we commuted together. I could always study at Babson on a weekend day or a weekday evening, and being with Victoria during the forty-five-minute commute (assuming normal traffic) and over a cup of coffee at Au Bon Pain at the Chestnut Hill Mall before her shift or during her break was an easily accessible pleasure. The mall was, after all, only a few miles from Babson.

In mid-November Missy invited us to her apartment in Charlestown for a party that included many members of the sales staff. It was a chilly and blustery night, and as always in greater Boston, finding a parking space was difficult. That area of Charlestown had no public parking garages at all despite its close proximity to the Bunker Hill Monument. After we had driven down several streets, Victoria suddenly exclaimed, "Oh, look! There's a spot!"

I slowed down and looked to where she was pointing. "I don't know," I said warily. Victoria had a certain innocence that was always endearing but on occasion landed us in hot water. "Someone has put two chairs in that space. Perhaps we shouldn't mess with them."

"Of course we should," Victoria insisted. "People can't save a parking space with chairs. It's not fair."

Before I could comment she had jumped out of the Ghia, placed the two chairs on the sidewalk, and was motioning me into the space.

Dutifully I complied, but when we arrived at Missy's apartment I told her what we had done. She blanched. "Get back there as fast as you can," she urged, "and move your car. And put the chairs back where you found them. If you don't, you'll find your tires slashed and your windshield bashed in."

I raced back to the car, grateful to find when I got there that "Boston Strong" punishment had not yet been meted out. It may not have been fair to put those chairs in that space, but it was how things were done—and no doubt how they still are done. Lesson learned, for us both.

⌒⌒

The holidays present a particular challenge for those who work in retail sales. The hours are long and grueling, and in Victoria's case they continued right up until six o'clock on Christmas Eve. Then, after Christmas and again after New Year's Eve, she had to deal with a tsunami of returns, exchanges, and gift cards. The chaos usually lasted until mid-January, which, perhaps not coincidentally, was when

December commission checks were distributed. When Victoria received her check in the mail, her eyes went wide before she handed it to me. When I saw the amount I had to sit down. It was more than three times as much as I had ever earned in a month as sales manager of a world-renowned publishing company. Of course, a check of that size came only one month a year—but, oh, what a month!

As an interesting footnote to the above, in November 1986 Victoria left Brooks Brothers not long before giving birth to our second son. She had been working part time for the previous two years but was still doing well financially because Brooks Brothers usually scheduled her on the weekends, when sales volume was highest and when I could stay home with our older son. In 1988, a year and a half later, Brooks Brothers was sold to Marks & Spencer, a British retailer seeking to expand into the U.S. clothing market. One of the first things Marks & Spencer did after taking control was to do away with sales commissions. Within two weeks nearly every sales representative at the Brooks Brothers store at the Chestnut Hill Mall had quit. Not surprisingly, sales of Brooks Brothers' merchandise plummeted nationally, forcing Marks & Spencer to sell the company in 2001 for one-third of what it had paid for it. Being penny-wise and pound-foolish is rarely a good idea, either in the living room or the boardroom.

Because Victoria had to work long hours during the holidays, we were unable to visit our families at that time, especially Victoria's family in Nebraska. So we began a routine of visiting my parents in Islamorada for a week in March and her family for a week during the summer. During those

several years, that was the extent of our overnight travel.
Business school even in 1983 was not cheap, and the honor
of paying the bills fell entirely to Victoria and me. Fortunately, during my first year of full-time study we had decent
cash flow and our Time Inc. stock to fall back on; but still
we needed to watch our nickels and dimes. Of course, visiting our parents had many benefits, and it was something we
always looked forward to doing.

I have one regret about those Nebraska trips: I wish
Victoria and I had managed to visit her dearest friend, Pat
Leavell, who lived a few hours' drive away in Iowa. It was
hard, always, because Granddaddy and Grandmommy
wanted as much time as possible with their beloved daughter and rolled out the red carpet to make certain that
happened. And, of course, we wanted to see Uncle Larry
and Aunt Pam and your cousins Benjamin and Peter, who
lived nearby in Schuyler. More often than not, Uncle Dick
and Aunt Mary and Kelli and Brian flew up from Scottsdale
to join the family fun.

So it was that before each trip to Howells, Victoria and
I vowed to drive the three hours to where Pat Leavell and
her husband, John, lived. As you now know, because we
have had the great pleasure and privilege of spending time
with Pat, she was your mother's closest friend growing up
in Howells and her closest friend in life. They got into all
kinds of mischief together and referred to themselves as
"sisters in spirit," sharing a bond that can never be broken
no matter how much time has elapsed. But family pressures
and pleasures always seemed to close in on Victoria whenever she and I ventured to Howells, so we deferred getting

together with Pat and John until "next time." Sadly, that next time never came. And now it's too late. Victoria has passed on and so has John.

The lesson here is obvious, and it is one that Victoria and I, and Pat and John, want you to heed very carefully.

⌇⌇

After reading our story thus far, you might have concluded that in those early years of our marriage Victoria and I lived for "big events"—an anniversary trip, a trip to visit our families, or an evening of dining and dancing at an elegant restaurant. If so, you have drawn the wrong conclusion. The truth is quite the opposite.

Victoria and I took just as much pleasure in doing little things together. Whether it was selecting seeds for our flower garden, going apple picking in the fall, going sledding or skating under a winter sun or moon (Victoria was an excellent skater), attending a Harvard versus Dartmouth football game, playing a round of miniature golf or shuffleboard, carving a pumpkin, or searching through local antique stores for a knick-knack to buy for the house, the point, always, was to be doing something together.

Often on a summer weekend we would rise early to try our luck at fishing for bluefish or striped bass off World's End in Hingham or Pemberton Point at the tip of Nantasket Peninsula. We rarely caught anything—more often than not we'd hook our lure onto a submerged log or some other obstruction and have to cut the line, thus ending our fishing expedition—but that didn't matter. We always had a thermos of Dunkin' Donuts coffee and either several of their doughnuts (whole wheat was Victoria's favorite) or muffins that Victoria had baked for the outing. Most mornings, two "skunked" fishermen would end up sitting side by side on the smooth rocks sipping coffee and munching on a pastry as we watched the sun rise above the Atlantic. Whether or not we got lucky, there was no such thing as a bad fishing trip.

Victoria's *joi de vivre* was in evidence at every holiday, even before you boys came along and when she was working long hours. Christmas was her favorite, especially when you boys were young, although as the years sped by, both Thanksgiving and Easter made ever-stronger showings— perhaps because they too are family-oriented holidays but without all the marketing hype that so demeans the true message of Christmas. Victoria celebrated even minor holidays in traditional fashion. After we moved to Hingham, for example, she would make a number of May baskets on the first day of May and fill them with flowers and homemade goodies to leave at the homes of our neighbors and close friends. The tradition of May Day baskets is for the giver to set the basket on the doorstep, ring the doorbell, and then run away before the recipient can catch you, because if you're caught, a kiss must be exchanged. I doubt any of our neighbors knew that tradition, and if certain ones had known, it would have made Victoria run away that much faster! In any event, to our knowledge no one else did this sort of thing in Hingham or anywhere else we ever lived, or understood why Victoria was doing it. But again, that didn't matter. Making and distributing the baskets gave Victoria pleasure, and the recipients of the baskets loved them. If ever there was a person who embodied the biblical message in Acts 20:35 that it is more blessed to give than to receive, that person is your mother.

Of course, the giving varied according to the giver and the recipient. In my family, after my sisters and I reached a certain age my parents didn't make much ado over our birthdays. The one exception was my father's birthday, which fell on the Fourth of July. It was a date on which we all tried to be together as a family to honor Pappy and give him joke gifts. For example, for his ninetieth birthday Victoria and I presented him—to his great delight—with a bottle of Johnny Walker Black with one of Harrison's baby bottle nipples taped to the top. Otherwise, birthdays were acknowledged by a telephone call, if my sisters or I were away from home, or a toast if we happened to be at home. As for Mirr, she wanted little to do with her own birthday. Advancing age was a sensitive issue to her.

That was not the case in Victoria's family, and it was not true for us after Victoria and I were married. Birthdays were nigh sacred events to her, and for weeks before every July sixteenth, Victoria anticipated with great relish all the pomp and ceremony of balloons, presents, and breakfast in bed. I always tried to make the day live up to her expectations. On her first birthday after we moved to Hingham, however, I committed a serious error. Victoria had let it be known that she would like to have an electric can opener for the kitchen. Aha, I thought. Her birthday is coming up and I will give her one as a gift! As it turned out, that was a very, very bad idea (and being an author and editor, I don't use the word "very" very often). Mind you, I also gave her other gifts that were far more personal and feminine. But for years thereafter Victoria would not let me forget that I had once committed the grievous offense of giving her an electric can opener for her birthday.

So, boys, take a tip from your old man. If you need an electric can opener for your kitchen, go out and buy one. But don't ever, *ever* contemplate giving one to your beloved for her birthday.

⌒

Perhaps the best illustration of our love of doing little things together requires me to fast-forward our story to 2009, when our world upended and came crashing down upon us. To conserve money in the midst of the chaos I closed my office in downtown Minneapolis and moved it into our home. Among other benefits of that decision, I got to spend much more time with Victoria each day. In short order we developed a routine that saw us each doing our own thing in the morning before meeting for lunch—either at home or at least once a week at D'Amico's restaurant, our favorite eatery, where Victoria was so beloved that the staff was always giving us free drinks or desserts, and sometimes entire meals. (How beloved was she? D'Amico's insisted on catering Victoria's memorial service at no profit to them, even though several hundred people were in attendance.)

After lunch we would go food shopping at Byerly's for the evening meal, return home to put those groceries away, and then drive out to pick up Harrison from college. After that, depending on work obligations, we might take a walk by a lake or tackle a game or two of Jumbles before settling in at six o'clock by the fire, a ritual we followed every day of the year, the heat of summer notwithstanding, thanks to the benefice of air-conditioning. There we would sip wine and talk and plan and reminisce until jungle drums erupted upstairs, announcing that you boys were hungry for dinner.

One day we were running late to pick up Harrison. No doubt the staff at Byerly's was hindering Victoria's progress up and down the aisles because they all wanted to say hello. (In Byerly's and elsewhere I was known simply as "Victoria's husband.") We finally managed to get home and into the kitchen with the groceries, whereupon I said, "Look, Dearheart, why don't I run down and pick up Harrison while you put away the food?"

"No," she said, "I want to come with you."

"That's fine," I countered. "But why? I'll be back in twenty or thirty minutes."

Her answer will forever pull at my heart. She said: "Because that means we will have twenty or thirty more minutes together today."

What do you say to a woman who says something like that to you after almost thirty-three years of marriage?

"I love you" is a good start. But that's all it is. A start.

Chapter 11

In the last few years I have described my life as a book with
thirty-five chapters, each chapter being a year in which I
knew your mother. Nearly thirty-four of those chapters are
years I spent as her husband. The years preceding those
chapters form the preface of my life's story. My life now is
the epilogue. Epilogues can be both long and creative, but
frankly, I have no interest in prolonging the epilogue of my
life for any longer than is necessary—meaning, any longer
than I am able to maintain an active and meaningful role
in your lives and the lives of your children. As soon as I
am unable to do that, I am more than ready to go. Why?
Because the first person to greet me on the other side will
be your mother. How do I know this? Among other reasons,
on my birthday six months after she died, she told me so.

But that is the subject of another book.

In 1983 we focused our attention on Hingham. Victoria
became involved in several local organizations in addi-

tion to the Junior League of Boston. One such organization was the Hingham Newcomers' Club. Soon after we moved to Hingham, three representatives of the club came to our door. One of them was toting a big wicker basket full of homemade foods and, more important, pamphlets and other information describing various churches, town ordinances and offices, and volunteer opportunities as well as lists of South Shore physicians, pediatricians, restaurants, movie theaters, and the like. Victoria was so impressed with the kindness and generosity of these women that she immediately volunteered her services on days she was not working.

As an interesting sidebar to the above, many old-line Hingham residents considered anyone a "newcomer" whose family had not lived in Hingham for at least three generations. That my direct ancestor, Thomas Hammond, had sailed from Portsmouth, England, to Hingham in 1649 apparently didn't count: perhaps because he had the audacity to move from Hingham to Newtowne, as Cambridge was called back then. Victoria and I were definitely newcomers. But so were most of our friends. And there was no social penalty for being of such lowly status. I suspect the old "bluestockings" simply enjoyed savoring their exalted South Shore heritage as they smugly sipped their sherry or martinis in their homes perched high on a hill overlooking Hingham Bay. Certainly all of them we met took to Victoria with no less enthusiasm and admiration than everyone else.

Somewhat ironically, in the mid-1980s I was invited to serve on a committee overseeing the publication of an official town history of Hingham titled *All Is Not Changed*. The book's two authors were highly competent researchers and writers, and it's always a privilege to work with people who know their business. Also serving on the committee were several town leaders and an editor I had worked with at Little, Brown. Victoria attended a number of weekly meetings as an interested observer, and she was always welcomed because of what she brought with her: her personality, ideas, and treats to share with everyone present. When the book was completed and published, Victoria and I were still newcomers, but we knew more about the history of Hingham than 99 percent of its residents!

Another close affiliation we made soon after moving to Hingham was with St. John's Episcopal Church. While living in Washington and in Boston we had attended a number of different churches, both Episcopal and Catholic, our favorite being Trinity Church in Boston's Back Bay. The denomination didn't matter much; Victoria and I both believed that what was important was worshiping God and giving Him thanks for our lives and marriage, whatever the venue. No church or sect has it all right, and none has it all wrong. The reason we chose St. John's was because many of our friends attended that church and we truly respected the rector, Father Robert Edson—now retired but still a close friend of our family. Also, attached to the church but managed separately from it was an attractive nursery school for prekindergarten children. Being in close proximity to its physical grounds and playground kept alive the dream of our own children someday attending St. John's Nursery School and playing on that playground. As it turned out, all three of you did.

Of course, it is the people who live there who make any community viable. And Hingham had and has more than its fair share of good people. When we first moved to Hingham we were warned that many residents could be stand-offish. If that was true, we never experienced it. Right from the get-go we made many friends of all ages and of various attachments to Hingham, from fifth-generation residents to newcomers just like us.

Much of the credit for that goes, of course, to Victoria. The warmth of her smile could melt the ice of a glacier and the heart of a socially prominent dowager. A common connector between married couples is children, but in 1983 we had no children. We still prayed daily for that blessing, but even without that immediate bond among adult strangers, Victoria amassed a number of friends within a remarkably short span of time. On weekends, and even during the week, our social calendar was demanding. Hingham quickly became our home, and not just because our house was located at 33 Lafayette Avenue.

It probably won't surprise you boys to learn that during those early years of our marriage your mother could kick up her heels as high as the best of them. She often tried to project an image of herself as the prim, proper, and punctilious Alpha Delta Pi sorority sister at the University of Nebraska who studied voraciously, and the no-nonsense art student at the Kansas City Art Institute who rarely partied and brooked no distractions from her work. You bought none of it. And you were wise not to.

I vividly recall the evening Victoria enjoyed a "girls' night out" with three friends who were married and, like us, childless. Victoria was the last one to be picked up, and after what appeared to be some deliberation in Susan's car about the evening's agenda, they took off down Lafayette Avenue. It turned out to be a late evening. Midnight was approaching when I saw the lights of Susan's car in our driveway.

"Nice evening?" I asked Victoria as she walked into the kitchen a few moments later.

"Yes," she said. "It was quite nice."

"Where did you end up going?"

"Jake's."

"Good choice." Jake's seafood restaurant in Hull was one of our favorite eateries on the South Shore. Most of the seafood the restaurant served was locally caught. "What did you have?"

Victoria recounted a seafood order that had apparently been reinforced by ample quantities of spirits—and I'm not referring to high spirits! It was not what she said that made me think so; it was how she said it. She wasn't meeting my gaze, and her voice was excessively casual—the voice of a child caught with her hand in the cookie jar.

"Okay," I said into the ensuing silence. "Out with it. I know you well enough to know that I haven't heard the entire story."

She gave me a sheepish grin. "No, you haven't."

"Well?" I pressed. "What part haven't I heard?"

"The worst part. We were asked to leave."

My jaw dropped. "Asked to *leave*? *You*? In heaven's name *why*?"

"We started dancing on the tables," Victoria blurted out.

I suppressed a smile. I was accustomed to Victoria's occasional shenanigans, but this was one for the books—

I should say, for the book. "All *four* of you were dancing on the tables?" I asked with mock incredulity.

"Not Peggy," Victoria replied softly. "She tried to, but she had more to drink than the rest of us. She fell over trying to climb up."

"Was she hurt?"

"No. Just embarrassed."

"I can imagine. Was there any damage to the tables?"

"I don't think so. We took off our shoes first. And I don't think there were any other patrons left at the time. Well, maybe one or two. The manager told us he wanted to close up, so we left and walked around outside for a while before Susan drove us home."

"Good idea. Was the manager mad at you?"

"I don't know. Carol said she saw him smiling at someone as we left. So I assume not. We'll have to see. I think he knows who I am."

"I'd wager he knew who you are long before tonight. But in any case," I added, "he surely knows who you are now." I wasn't angry with her. Not at all. Inside I was thinking, with a burst of pride, "*That's* my girl!"

The next day I tested the waters by calling Jake's to make a reservation for that Friday evening. When I deliberately put the reservation in Victoria's name, I didn't hear any gasps or giggles on the other end of the line. So far, so good. Then, to our surprise, when we arrived at the restaurant we were shown to the best table in the house, the one with a panoramic view of Hull Bay at sunset. Minutes later the manager stopped by our table holding a glass of chardonnay.

"I believe this is your preferred wine, Mrs. Hammond,"

he exclaimed as he placed the glass in front of Victoria. He gave me a wink and strode off.

As Victoria flashed me one of her glorious smiles, I couldn't help imagining what would have happened to me if I had been the one dancing on those tables. No doubt I would have been tied up and dumped into the bay, there to serve as a feast for lobsters, crabs, and other bottom-feeding denizens of the deep.

No, boys, life is not always fair. But sometimes you don't care that it isn't. That memorable evening at Jake's is a good example.

◡◠

The summer of 1983 passed uneventfully for us, or so it seemed at its conclusion on Labor Day. Hingham is a popular place during the hot summer months because of its charm, its cozy and alluring shops, its seafaring history, and its proximity to Cape Cod, a mere forty-five minutes away down the Southeast Expressway (except on Friday afternoon and every evening, when that drive can take three hours or more). A highlight of every summer there is the Fourth of July parade. You remember it: a scene from a Norman Rockwell depiction of a quintessential New England extravaganza celebrating our independence from Great Britain. Of course, although it's rarely mentioned, many Hingham residents remained Tories—staunchly pro-English—throughout the duration of the Revolutionary War.

We had close friends who lived along the lower Main Street parade route, and each summer Jack and Kate hosted a barbeque to add to the festivities. Victoria and I

always made a day out of it, and we cherished every minute of that day. Even now the memories linger, continually
vying with so many others for my attention and my heart.

⌒〇

I took two courses during the first summer semester at Babson, thoroughly immersing myself in accounting and entrepreneurial finance. The second session I took off because
I wanted to devote more energy to my primary consulting
clients. Tim, Harry, and I had continued to meet on a routine
basis, often conducting our meetings over lunch at a fine
Boston restaurant. Tim's company had raised the desired capital and was soon to launch its first list of books, so there was
serious work to do. I confess to enjoying being back in the
world of business, especially now that the MBTA had seen fit
to launch a line of sleek high-speed commuter boats between
Hingham Shipyard and Rowes Wharf in Boston, departing
each location every thirty minutes during rush hours. Gone
for good was the old tub, as loyal and trustworthy (well, sort
of) as she may have been. She had been replaced by a most
agreeable commute that took a mere half hour, a magic
carpet ride that was sending South Shore housing prices
skyrocketing through the roof, or so realtors claimed.

"Get on the elevator," local real estate agents insisted.
"Whatever you do, don't get left behind. Buy anything in
Hingham, hold onto it until the short-term capital gains tax
no longer applies, and then sell it for a huge profit." What
they failed to mention, of course, is that sooner or later all
elevators reach the top floor, and from there they begin
their sorry slide back down toward the bottom floors.

In August of that summer of 1983 Victoria took a few days off from work and we drove to Hancock Point to visit my parents. Aside from enjoying the usual summer pursuits available on the coast of Maine, we enjoyed Pappy's newest addition to the property: a Jacuzzi installed at a spot affording a panoramic view of Frenchman Bay and the hills of Mount Desert Island three miles across it. After a day of sailing or hiking, it was pure hedonistic pleasure to join Pappy in the Jacuzzi in the late afternoon, knowing that cocktail hour was next on the agenda. But the best was yet to come. Later, within the cloak of night to ensure privacy, Victoria and I had the Jacuzzi entirely to ourselves, and that's when we made the best use of it.

Two months later, on a Friday (I remember it was Friday because I had no classes on Friday that semester), I was going in to Boston to confer with Tim and Harry. Victoria was off from work that day and had made arrangements to fulfill a Junior League obligation—or so she claimed. She offered to give me a ride to Hingham Shipyard on her way in and then pick me up at 5:30.

I also remember that it was a glorious mid-October day: cool with bright sunshine in a cloudless sky highlighting the brilliant autumn colors on the mainland and the Boston Harbor islands. During the commute back to Hingham I sat on the upper deck, as I preferred to do even in cool weather. I love the feel of sea air blowing against my face, and on that day the scenery on both sides of the boat truly was breathtaking.

As the boat slowly approached her berth at the shipyard and bumped up against it, I searched the large parking lot and the road leading in to the shipyard for the yellow Ghia. Not seeing it, I waited several minutes for the commuters belowdecks to disembark before I followed them onto the dock and up the gangway.

When I reached the platform and the ticket office, I saw Victoria slowly walking toward me. That by itself was unusual. Normally when she picked me up at the boat, she waited in the car for me to come to her.

"Hi," she said a bit too casually when we met halfway and stopped before each other. The last of the commuters on my boat had filed past, and we were alone on that patch of turf.

"Hi," I replied hesitantly. "How was your Junior League meeting?"

"There never was a Junior League meeting."

"But I thought you said . . . "

"I know what I said," Victoria interrupted with a smile. "I lied."

That statement was unprecedented. Victoria never lied. About anything. *Ever.* And yet here she was, standing before me, not only confessing to a fib but smiling about it.

There was nothing I could do but wait for her to continue. Which I knew she would do because I could see she was having trouble holding something in.

Suddenly she raised her hand to my cheek and kissed me full on the lips. Then she wrapped an arm around my neck, drawing me in closer, and shifted her lips to my ear. "I went to see Dr. Hernandez," she whispered, referring to her primary physician at New England OB-GYN Associates. "I'm pregnant."

I don't recall the first thing that went through my mind when she said that. But I do recall throwing my attaché case high into the air. And once I was sure that it wouldn't land on either of us or on someone else, I picked up Victoria and twirled her around and around and around, as though we were in some bizarre, out-of-control square dance. No doubt the commuters driving out of the shipyard thought we had gone half-mad as they took in the scene of a young woman being spun around in circles while shrieking and laughing uproariously.

If so, those onlookers would have been half right. We had gone *completely* mad. With joy.

Chapter 12

Victoria had made an appointment for us the next week to discuss matters with Dr. Vivian Hernandez. We had already decided not to share the joyous news with anyone until after the end of the first trimester, which would be in mid-November. The due date was Monday, May 21, so we felt we had plenty of time to plan. Of immediate interest on that day in the clinic was the ultrasound image of a tiny fetus already assuming human form. That was our son or daughter, and what we observed inspired a wave of complex emotions in us both. How anyone can look at such an image—more to the point, how anyone can be present at the birth of a child—and deny the love and omnipotence of God (or whatever name you prefer to apply to the Source) is beyond my ability to understand.

We did not know the baby's gender, nor did we want to until his or her birthday. But years earlier we had picked out the baby's name. If a girl, she would be named Katherine Bliss Hammond. Katherine was a preferred name on both sides of our family, and Bliss was the name of my beloved aunt who had died of cancer in her forties. If a boy, well, that too was a no-brainer. He would be named William Churchill Hammond IV—else William Churchill Hammond Jr. would have something to say on the matter, and that something would not be complimentary! But it was the name both Victoria and I would have selected in any event.

"Everything looks fine, Mr. and Mrs. Hammond," Dr. Hernandez assured us in her soothing yet highly professional tone. "Starting now, we will want to see you on a once-a-month basis, but of course you can make an additional appointment at any time should you feel the need to. And you can always call the clinic if you have questions or concerns. Do you have any questions for me now?"

It was rare for Victoria and me to be tongue-tied at the same time. But we were, still. The enormity of it all— together we had created a new life that we had just witnessed on a screen, a precious life that would henceforth define us as a couple and as a family—had rendered us momentarily speechless.

"Thank you, Doctor," I managed at length, adding, because I needed to add *something*, "What should we be doing now? What are the priorities beyond scheduling appointments?"

Dr. Hernandez gave me a warm smile. "Well, as I suggested to your wife last week, I urge you to enroll in a Lamaze class beginning in March. It's a five-week course. We are all depending on you to be an integral part of the process right up to and through the delivery. I think you will find these classes very beneficial. Otherwise, live your life as you normally would. Just be careful to avoid hard falls and go light on the wine. I recommend no more than two glasses a week."

"We will do that, Doctor," I said.

As Dr. Hernandez made to leave the examining room, she turned to look at me. "Mr. Hammond, may I tell you something?"

"Of course, Doctor."

"After I gave Mrs. Hammond the joyful news last week, we talked for a while. As an obstetrician I like to get to know a little about my patients and their family life. I will leave it to your wife to tell you the specifics of what we discussed, if she hasn't already. But what I can tell you based on what I heard from her then and from what I have observed here today is that you two have a very special bond. You will make wonderful parents because of your deep love for each other. I don't often see this level of commitment and devotion, and I congratulate you both for having achieved it. You are among the most fortunate of people, and your children will be the beneficiaries of that blessing."

For the second time that hour I was rendered speech-less. I could only nod at her in appreciation of what she had just said. She gave me a nod in acknowledgment and then another gentle smile. "We will take good care of your wife and child, I promise you, Mr. Hammond," she said before she walked out of the room and clicked the door shut behind her.

⌣◯

We called my parents at mid-afternoon on Thanksgiving Day. Normally they left Hancock Point for Islamorada in early December, but that year they had decided to fly south in mid-November. My mother preferred the searing heat of the Florida Keys to the freezing cold of Maine, and the decision, I suspect, was hers. As I said earlier, what my mother wanted, my mother usually got.

She answered the phone. After some preliminary conversation with me and with Victoria, who was on a separate phone in a different room, I asked Mirr if Pappy was there because we had something we wanted to tell them.

"He's here," Mirr said. "But he's practicing fly-casting out by the cove."

"Can you call him in?"

"Well," Mirr wavered, "you know your father. He doesn't like to be interrupted when he's practicing his fly-casting. Are you calling to wish us a happy Thanksgiving? If so, we were planning to call you this evening."

"Actually, no," I replied. "That's not it. We have another reason for calling, and Thanksgiving is the perfect day to tell you our news."

"What, then? Is it *that* important?"

"That would depend on whether or not Dad considers information about the pending birth of his first grandchild more important than cutting short a fly-casting session."

Despite myself I held my breath, because I knew my father so well. But I was determined that he was going to hear the news from us on that very day.

"Are you telling us . . . ? Mirr began hesitantly.

"Yes, we are. You're going to be grandparents. Get Dad, would you?"

As you remember, your grandmother was raised a proper Bostonian lady with the combination of old-school upbringing, Milton Academy, and Vassar exhorting her never to run except when exercising or to express undue sentiments unless in an emergency. But she threw all that to the wind as she bolted across the room, threw aside the sliding glass door with a loud bang, and cried out in a voice for all of Florida to hear, "Bill, get up here! *Immediately!*"

"I think we got to her," Victoria said to me over the extension. I could just imagine the smile on her face as she said that.

And she was right. We had gotten to her. As we also did to Pappy. I suffer no doubt that on that special Thanksgiving, cocktail hour for my parents started within two minutes of ending our conversation, the early hour be damned.

⁓

We waited to tell Victoria's parents until New Year's Day, when we could tell them in person. Since the first of December Victoria had had only one day off, so busy was the holiday season. Just before Christmas, when Victoria told the store manager that she was expecting, he insisted that she take some paid time off as soon as possible. (In 1984 Brooks Brothers was still privately owned. The Marks & Spencer management never would have been so accommodating.) So we flew to Omaha on the last flight out on New Year's Eve. Because the weather forecast in Nebraska called for cold and snow, we stayed the night at the Airport

Ramada before picking up a rental car and driving the two hours to Howells on New Year's Day.

To say that Granddaddy and Grandmommy were pleased with the news would be a pathetic understatement. Grandmommy knew exactly what was afoot the moment we walked into the house because Victoria was already "showing." (Granddaddy, like most men, was slower to notice the subtle changes—or perhaps worried about confusing pregnancy with weight gain.) For the next week they fawned over us, spoiling us rotten in the process. It was a week filled with warmth and love, never mind the frigid conditions outdoors. We even had a second Christmas because the tree was still up with our neatly wrapped presents beneath it. Being the incredibly generous man that he was, Granddaddy was no doubt imagining future Christmases when a third crop of grandchildren would be running and screeching around the house, excited to the brink of delirium by the sight of so many presents flooding the living room floor, the majority earmarked for them.

Once we were back in Hingham, word about the upcoming blessed event spread quickly, as it tends to do. Friends called or stopped by, and invitations for dinner started pouring in. First in line to congratulate us was Paul Morgan, who set to work right away to transform the guest room into a nursery. I don't know how many of Paul's clients were inconvenienced (or made furious) by the announcement of our pregnancy and Paul's subsequent attention to our home; I suspect there were many, but as always we appreciated beyond words his enthusiasm and suggestions, and especially his friendship.

The ample time we thought we had until May 21 began to melt away as quickly as the last remnants of snow on a warm spring day. Victoria's monthly check-ups at the clinic continued to go well—so well, in fact, that her doctor saw no reason for us not to continue living life as we normally did. So we decided to do just that—or at least to live life as we once had—by taking a train down to New York during my spring break in March. We knew this would the last time, barring a calamity we did not want to contemplate, that we would be traveling without children either accompanying us or waiting for us to return home.

Because Saint Nick, like me, was no longer employed within the Time Inc. empire, we could not stay for free at the Time-Life suite at the Windsor Hotel. We would be paying for our own lodging, which meant that we would stay in New York for only two nights—the most we felt we could comfortably afford. I surveyed a number of hotels by phone—back then there was no Internet (imagine!) and therefore no hotwire.com or hotels.com—and found that the one with the most reasonable daily rate was the Park Lane, a lovely hostelry on Central Park South. As was the case with all of our trips, we had a memorable time during that short but event-filled adventure. Highlights included a performance of the famed Broadway play *La Cage aux Folles*, a tour of Wall Street and the New York Stock Exchange, and dinner at Asti's, a restaurant in Greenwich Village. The majority of Asti's waiters were professional opera singers, and they routinely performed for patrons. I had gone there several times in earlier years with Lance and with friends, and I was eager to introduce the restaurant to

Victoria. She absolutely loved it, pronouncing it, years later, as one of our best evenings out ever. (Sadly, Asti's closed its doors for good in 2000. Although Victoria and I had dined there only once, we both felt as though we had lost a special friend.)

On Monday, March 26, we began a weekly regimen of Lamaze classes at the Hingham Community Center, which was less than a quarter mile from our house on Lafayette Avenue. The Lamaze Technique, as it is more formally known, was devised by a French obstetrician and is an alternative to constant medical attention during the birthing process. The technique focuses on breathing to manage pain and promote comfort. As I recall, there were quite a number of other couples taking the class with us, several of whom we already knew and all of whom quickly became close friends. Sharing a life-defining event such as preparing for the birth of a child naturally draws people together. I remain in contact with one of those couples even to this day.

Victoria had notified Brooks Brothers that her last day of work before taking maternity leave would be Friday, May 12. That was three days after my last final exam for the semester, and it would give us, or so we presumed, almost ten days before our due date to make last-minute preparations and tie up loose strings. That process had started weeks earlier, of course. In addition to seeing as many friends as possible before the big day, there were many other events and appointments to schedule, not the least of which were interviews with prospective pediatricians. Victoria and I met with a number of them before settling on South Shore Pediatrics in South Weymouth.

Whether the occasion was to interview the kindly "Dockie Cox," as you boys came to call him, or a visit to the dentist or the eye doctor or New England OB-GYN Associates, the day was always capped with a visit to an ice cream parlor. Much has been written about pregnant women's cravings for odd foods at odd hours. But there was nothing odd about Victoria's requests. She wanted ice cream and lots of it, any flavor, at *all* hours. Brigham's in downtown Hingham was her preferred source, and the good people working there saw a lot of me during those first four months of 1984. No doubt they had to order in extra tubs of ice cream to meet the demand from their favorite customer. And no doubt senior management had conferred more than once with medical experts to determine a way to keep the pregnancy going!

Everything went according to plan until the early-morning hours of May 15, when Victoria told me that she was feeling what she thought could be contractions. In Lamaze class we had learned, to the extent possible, how to differentiate between real and false contractions, and what to do for each.

"This must be a false alarm," Victoria assured me. "We're still a week away from my due date."

Because your mother was an eternal optimist, I had learned to tread carefully on what I suspected might be thin ice.

"How far apart are the contractions?" I asked her.

"I think about every fifteen minutes."

"We need to be more precise," I said, the business manager in me coming through. "I'll get the timer."

So we started timing the contractions, both in length and in intervals apart. The initial intervals were indeed about fifteen minutes, and the contractions were lasting a minute or so. But the intervals started to narrow to twelve and then to ten minutes.

"I'm calling the clinic," I said. "We can't take any chances."

I placed the call, talked with the nurse on duty, and reported to Victoria, who was sitting at the kitchen table: "They want us to come in. I'll get your bag"—packed two weeks earlier—"and start the car."

I was quickly becoming a Nervous Nellie (or a Worried Willie), but Victoria didn't blink.

"Do you think we could stop in Wellesley on the way there?" she asked nonchalantly.

"*In Wellesley?* Why would you want to stop in Wellesley?"

"The Junior League Showhouse is there, and this may be my only chance to see it."

I went slack-jawed. "You're joking, right?"

"No. I'm serious. We'll have time. It's only a little out of the way and won't take long."

Talk about cool under fire! Good grief! "Request denied, my love," I said unequivocally. "We're going straight to the clinic."

And straight to the clinic we went, as quickly and as carefully as I could navigate Route 3 into Boston. Fortunately, it was late morning and traffic was light. Of greater fortune was the fact that the clinic was located directly across Francis Street from Brigham & Women's Hospital, because as soon as we walked into it, Victoria's water broke. There she stood at the doorway before gawking staff and patients, her pants soaked, actually laughing at the way she saw herself in her mind's eye.

A nurse came up to us. "There's no need for the doctor to examine her here," she said, confirming the blatantly obvious. "Let's get your wife across the street."

An orderly produced a wheelchair, and the nurse ran outside to summon a police officer to escort us safely into the hospital lobby. I pushed the wheelchair before yielding it to a nurse's assistant at the reception desk. While I produced identification and insurance cards, Victoria was wheeled down the hall and up the elevator to the maternity ward. I followed minutes later, identified myself as the husband and father at the nurses' station, and was told to change into scrubs before entering the room in which Victoria was being tended to.

Victoria was dressed in a hospital gown and was half-sitting up in bed when I came in. Two attendants were scurrying about, hooking up monitors and generally setting the stage for what appeared to be a fast-paced birthing process. Victoria smiled at me when I walked to her bedside and kissed her brow. She was in pain, there was no doubt about that, but the only other thing I clearly remember from that blur of hard emotions is that I had forgotten everything I had learned in the Lamaze classes. Victoria apparently had forgotten her lessons too, because when we tried to reconstruct the breathing exercises she just shook her head in frustration.

During the blissful thirty-four years I lived with your mother I never heard her curse or use foul language—and I mean *not once*, even on this day when she was experiencing one of the most grueling and painful ordeals a woman can endure. She was beyond brave; she was heroic. We tried breathing exercises and we held each other's eyes through it all, even when, to my great relief, Dr. Finlayson (a partner in the clinic) came into the room, examined Victoria, and announced that things were good to go and should be happening in rapid-fire action.

Then, at 3:45 in the afternoon, approximately three hours after we entered the hospital, I saw Victoria close her eyes in a fierce squint and I felt her push with all her might. Moments later I heard a loud cry—not from Victoria but from you, Churchill. You had made your appearance on the world stage, and you were making sure everyone within earshot was aware of your glorious entry.

While Dr. Finlayson was tending to Victoria—with the quip, "The next time you are approaching your due date, Mrs. Hammond, I suggest you have a helicopter standing by on your lawn"—a nurse cleaned up our baby, wrapped him in a prewarmed blanket, and placed him gently in my arms. I will never forget the moment when for the first time I gazed down upon my son, who returned my gaze with a look of curiosity mixed with utter indifference. Nor will I forget the moment when I placed Churchill on his mother's chest and she began gently massaging his back as I stood at bedside, happily watching as the sacred bond between mother and child took root before my eyes.

When she shifted her loving gaze up to mine, I was reminded, once again but never with more fervency, that indeed I had won life's greatest lottery. And because I had, so had you boys. And so have your unborn children, and on and on down through future generations of Hammonds, each one imbued with the blessings and genes of a dear women who has defined my life just as she will define my eternity.

It is the way of the universe and it is the way of God's love, His greatest gift to us all.

Epilogue

A week before Christmas in 1988 I returned to our home in Hingham following a dinner engagement in Boston. The air was frosty and snow was falling gently, a perfect setting to highlight the holiday decorations tastefully displayed throughout the "quintessential New England town at Christmas."

After parking the car in the garage, I walked into the house through the dimly lit kitchen and removed my outer coat, blazer, and shoes. As I loosened my tie, I listened for any telltale sounds. Hearing nothing beyond distant music, I walked down the front hallway and entered the living room on the left. That room, too, was dimly lit. The only lamp burning was on an end table beside the sofa, its soft glow reinforced by the lights of the Christmas tree and the glow of the still-flaming birch logs in the hearth.

Victoria was sitting on the sofa with Churchill on her right and Brooks on her left. (Harrison, you were still a dream not to be realized for another three years.) Both boys were dressed in one-piece, zip-up pajamas with feet, and both were asleep. So was Victoria. On her lap was an open

Christmas storybook that she had been reading to her sons. In the background WJIB in Boston was playing Christmas music—not the "Rocking around the Christmas Tree" and "Santa Baby" nonsense played far too often during the holidays, but classic Christmas carols such as "O Little Town of Bethlehem" and "Good King Wenceslas" sung by the full choir at King's Chapel in Cambridge, England. At just the moment I walked into the room, the radio station started playing "Silent Night."

I tiptoed over to the sofa and switched off the light. Then I tossed another log on the fire and sat down in a wingback chair facing the sofa across from a coffee table on which was neatly stacked the day's harvest of Christmas cards, which Victoria and I would open together after you boys were asleep. The lights on the Christmas tree twinkled, and the birch wood in the fireplace popped agreeably as I sat there in the cozy silence and stared lovingly at my family.

As though sensing my presence, Victoria opened her eyes and smiled at me. For a span of time impossible to measure—as I said earlier, when I was with your mother, time often assumed a different dimension—we sat across from each other, our hearts and souls engaged in a lively dialogue requiring no words.

Suddenly Churchill stirred, opened his eyes, and said, "Hi, Daddy." That set Brooks to yawning and rubbing his eyes. It was past time to put you boys to bed.

Victoria picked up Brooks and I picked up Churchill and together we walked upstairs. Victoria went into Brooks' room and I took Churchill into his room directly across the hall. A few minutes later, after I had tucked Churchill into bed and we had said our prayers (or I said them; Churchill was already asleep), I stepped back out into the hall.

At that same instant, Victoria stepped out of Brooks' room. Our eyes locked, and without uttering a word or employing any sort of body language we came together in a warm embrace, as though it were the most natural act in the world—which for us it was. Then we started slow dancing together, without music, just as we had those many years ago in a restaurant perched high atop a Kansas City skyscraper.

"I love you, Dearheart," Victoria whispered in my ear.

"I love you," I whispered in hers. "And I will forever."

And ever.

World without end.

Amen.

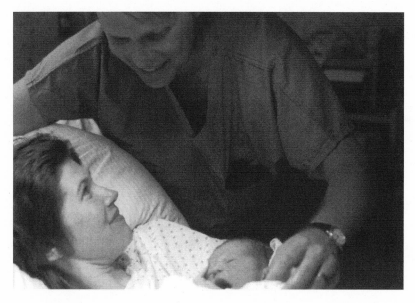

Brigham and Women's Hospital
May 15, 1984

This book is dedicated to establishing a scholarship in Victoria's name at the Kansas City Art Institute.

If you find this book meaningful to you, and if you are moved to do so, please make a donation directly to the Kansas City Art Institute, from which Victoria graduated in 1973. All donations are tax deductible and will be used to establish the Victoria K. Hammond Scholarship. Victoria and I are grateful to you for your kind consideration of this request.

Please send your donation to:

Advancement Office
Kansas City Art Institute
4415 Warwick Boulevard
Kansas City, MO 64111

Be sure to specify
"The Victoria K. Hammond Scholarship"
on your check.

Thank you.